THE 30-DAY PRODUCTIVITY PLAN - VOLUME II

30 MORE BAD HABITS THAT ARE SABOTAGING YOUR TIME MANAGEMENT - AND HOW TO OVERCOME THEM ONE DAY AT A TIME!

DAMON ZAHARIADES

CONTENTS

OTHER BOOKS BY DAMON ZAHARIADES

~

The P.R.I.M.E.R. Goal Setting Method: The Only Goal Achievement Guide You'll Ever Need!

An elegant 6-step system for achieving extraordinary results in every area of your life!

~

80/20 Your Life! How To Get More Done With Less Effort And Change Your Life In The Process!

Achieve more, create more, and enjoy more success - while taking less action! It's time to 80/20 your life!

~

The Joy Of Imperfection: A Stress-Free Guide To Silencing Your Inner Critic, Conquering Perfectionism, and Becoming The Best Version Of Yourself!

Is perfectionism causing you to feel stressed, irritated, and chronically unhappy? Here's how to silence your inner critic, embrace imperfection, and live without fear!

The Art Of Saying NO: How To Stand Your Ground, Reclaim Your Time And Energy, And Refuse To Be Taken For Granted (Without Feeling Guilty!)

Are you fed up with people taking you for granted? Learn how to set boundaries, stand your ground, and inspire others' respect in the process!

The Procrastination Cure: 21 Proven Tactics For Conquering Your Inner Procrastinator, Mastering Your Time, And Boosting Your Productivity!

Do you struggle with procrastination? Discover how to take quick action, make fast decisions, and finally overcome your inner procrastinator!

Morning Makeover: How To Boost Your Productivity, Explode Your Energy, and Create An Extraordinary Life - One Morning At A Time!

Would you like to start each day on the right foot? Here's how to create quality morning routines that set you up for more daily success!

$$\sim$$

Fast Focus: A Quick-Start Guide To Mastering Your Attention, Ignoring Distractions, And Getting More Done In Less Time!

Are you constantly distracted? Does your mind wander after just a few minutes? Learn how to develop laser-sharp focus!

$$\sim$$

Small Habits Revolution: 10 Steps To Transforming Your Life Through The Power Of Mini Habits!

Got 5 minutes a day? Use this simple, effective plan for creating any new habit you desire!

$$\sim$$

The 30-Day Productivity Plan: Break The 30 Bad Habits That Are Sabotaging Your Time Management - One Day At A Time!

Need a daily action plan to boost your productivity? This 30-day guide is the solution to your time management woes!

**The Time Chunking Method: A 10-Step Action Plan For
Increasing Your Productivity**

It's one of the most popular time management strategies used
today. Double your productivity with this easy 10-step system.

**Digital Detox: The Ultimate Guide To Beating
Technology Addiction, Cultivating Mindfulness, and
Enjoying More Creativity, Inspiration, And Balance In
Your Life!**

Are you addicted to Facebook and Instagram? Are you obsessed
with your phone? Use this simple, step-by-step plan to take a
technology vacation!

For a complete list, please visit

http://artofproductivity.com/my-books/

YOUR FREE GIFT

≈

As my way of saying thank you for purchasing *The 30-Day Productivity Plan - Volume II*, I'd like to offer you my 40-page action guide titled *Catapult Your Productivity! The Top 10 Habits You Must Develop To Get More Things Done.*

It's in PDF format, so you can print it out easily and read it at your leisure. This guide will show you how to develop core habits that'll help you to get more done in less time.

You can grab your copy by clicking on the following link and joining my mailing list:

http://artofproductivity.com/free-gift/

You'll also receive periodic tips for overcoming procrastination, developing effective morning routines, sharpening your focus, and much more!

Now, let's jump in. We have a lot to cover in *The 30-Day Productivity Plan - Volume II.*

PREFACE

We should strive to develop and maintain good productivity habits. They allow us to squeeze more out of our day. They help us to work more efficiently, and in so doing help us to get more things done in less time.

But as important as it is to develop *good* habits, it's the *bad* habits that prevent us from working productively and managing our time. Whether they stem from poor impulse control or a lifetime of reinforcement is irrelevant. The important thing is that we identify these habits, acknowledge their adverse effects on our time, and take measures to overcome them.

That's the purpose of this book.

You may have read my previous book *The 30-Day*

Productivity Plan - Volume I. It highlights 30 bad habits that sabotage our ability to get things done. It also provided step-by-step instructions for curbing each of them. *The 30-Day Productivity Plan - Volume II* continues that theme. We're going to cover 30 *more* bad habits that may be holding you back and preventing you from squeezing maximum value from each day.

The format remains the same. This book, like the previous one, is organized into 30 chapters. Each chapter is short and to the point, and contains *actionable* advice on how to break the bad habit under examination.

Keep in mind, the "30-day" protocol is merely a matter of convention. In truth, it doesn't matter whether you work on changing one bad habit a day or one bad habit a week. The important thing - and this will ultimately determine how much value you get from this book - is to take *consistent action* toward breaking the habits.

I'll show you how to do so. As in football, you're holding the playbook. Everything you need to succeed is detailed in the following pages. But it's up to you to execute the plays. And if you discover that one or more fail to work for you, it's up to you to try different ones.

Developing *good* habits requires taking purposeful action on a daily basis. The same is true for breaking *bad* habits. You possess the playbook. The rest boils down to implementation.

Let's get started by taking a look at why bad habits are so hard to break.

Damon Zahariades

http://www.ArtOfProductivity.com

WHY BAD HABITS ARE SO HARD
TO BREAK

~

Many of our daily actions stem from learned habits. These habits are programmed into our psyches via past repetitive action. Good and bad, they activate learned routines, compelling us to respond automatically to internal and external cues. In the process, they dictate our daily experience.

For example, suppose you're a stress eater. During periods of high stress, you instinctively reach for junk food, such as ice cream, candy bars, or cookies. Years of responding to stress in this manner has caused the habit to become deeply ingrained within your brain. Your response is automatic.

It's often difficult to recognize bad habits because they're invisible to us. Daily application has entrenched them in our lives to the point that we hardly notice them. For example, we impulsively visit Facebook, YouTube, and Instagram with little thought regarding the time we waste in the process. We turn on the television, just for a few minutes of leisure, and are surprised to find ourselves binge-watching shows on Netflix rather than getting work done. We automatically say "yes" to people without considering how doing so will negatively impact our productivity.

We do these things over and over, day in and day out. These habits, or learned routines, are ingrained in our minds. They're automatic responses to internal and external cues.

The problem is, if a bad habit is essentially a reflex, and it's invisible to us due to continual application (sometimes for years on end), how can we overcome it?

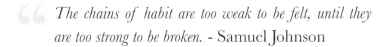

The chains of habit are too weak to be felt, until they are too strong to be broken. - Samuel Johnson

Is Willpower The Solution?

When we set out to break bad habits, it's easy to be seduced into thinking that all we need is willpower. That is, if we possess enough mental grit, we can resist our impulses. But you know from experience that willpower alone won't suffice. It never does.

There's a simple reason: ego depletion.

When we wake up each morning, we possess a "full tank" of willpower. It's a limited resource that we use up as the day progresses. Each time we make a decision that forces us to exert self-control (e.g. work instead of watching Netflix), we expend a little bit of it. Each decision causes the gauge on our willpower tank to move incrementally from "full" to "empty." As your willpower is depleted, it becomes more difficult to exert self-control when making decisions.

Imagine waking up in the morning after eight hours of quality sleep. You feel energized and ready to tackle the day. Your willpower tank is full, and thus making decisions that require self-control is relatively easy. For example, you prepare a healthy breakfast rather than eat a few donuts.

Now imagine it's the *end* of the day. You're tired, stressed, and mildly irritated. Because you've been making decisions and employing self-control for several hours, your tank is empty. Resisting temptations is much more difficult. You're more vulnerable to them.

This is the reason we can't rely on willpower alone to overcome our bad habits. Doing so never works. Even if we manage to curb unhealthy routines for a few days, we're likely to return to them when our willpower tank is empty.

This book is going to show you a much better way to change unhealthy, unproductive routines. We're going to follow a simple, step-by-step action plan for each of the 30 bad habits profiled in the following pages. These plans are designed to *replace* unproductive practices with productive ones.

Willpower will be a factor, of course (it always is when

we change our habitual processes). The important thing is, we're not going to rely on it.

Is It Really That Important To Break "Tiny" Bad Habits?

Some bad habits seem inconsequential, especially when compared to those that can have truly catastrophic results. It's tempting to ignore them and tell ourselves that maintaining a few small vices won't kill us. For example, compared to smoking, gambling, and illicit drug use, perfectionism, multitasking, and spending too much time on Facebook seem almost trivial.

But unhealthy routines have a *cumulative* effect on us. They add up, and in aggregate can throw our lives into disarray.

Have you ever felt as if your day was spiraling out of control, and you were unable to identify the reason? It's possible you were experiencing the cumulative impact of multiple "tiny" bad habits.

Imagine this scenario: in the morning, while lying in bed, you keep hitting the snooze button on your alarm clock. This causes you to arrive late at your job, increasing your stress. Then, your inclination to say yes to coworkers who approach you for help overburdens you with work. Meanwhile, your susceptibility to distractions (hello Facebook!) prevents you from completing tasks on your to-do list. And throughout the day, your aversion to writing down details, preferring to keep everything in your head, causes important items to slip through the cracks.

By the time you leave your job, you're frustrated, exhausted, and disappointed. The day was a disaster, but you can't seem to place your finger on the reason.

In this case, the frustration, exhaustion, and disappointment stem from the consequences of maintaining numerous unhealthy, unproductive behaviors. Each behavior is arguably small. By itself, it may seem inconsequential. But *cumulatively*, they have a major impact.

The premise of *The 30-Day Productivity Plan - Volume II* (as well as the book that preceded it) is that curbing numerous small routines that waste our time and energy can have a remarkable effect on our productivity. To that end, as we did in the previous volume, we're going to take a close look at 30 such habits with the goal of overcoming them. Each one may seem tiny on its own. But I guarantee you'll see a vast improvement in your productivity, effectiveness, and confidence once you've curbed them.

How To Get The Most Out Of This Book

If you've read any of my other books, you know I'm not a fan of untempered cheerleading. It's important to remain enthusiastic about the changes you want to make in your life. But in my opinion, such enthusiasm has limited value unless it's accompanied by daily application. So while I'll encourage you throughout this book, the main focus will be on *actionable* advice.

You also know I rarely dedicate significant space to the deep psychology of why we do the things we do. Such material *is* important. But in my opinion, it's mostly so in the preparation of creating step-by-step plans for changing our behaviors. That is, we don't need to know the psychology behind habit change to transform our lives. However, we *do* need to take daily action to realize that transformation. Action trumps investigation.

As I mentioned in the preface, don't put too much stock in the "30-day" part of this book's title. Work at a pace that suits you. Making a *commitment* to breaking bad habits is more important than meeting an arbitrary deadline. As they say, life is a marathon, not a sprint.

Here's the approach I recommend:

First, read through the table of contents so you'll be familiar with the material we'll cover in *The 30-Day Productivity Plan - Volume II.*

Second, skim each chapter. Get a feel for the format. You'll already be familiar with the format if you've read the preceding title (*The 30-Day Productivity Plan - Volume I*).

Third, note which habits are most critical to you. It's unlikely you're struggling with all 30. And even if you are, you're probably not struggling with them to the same degree. So pick and choose based on which ones are having the greatest impact on your life. For example, you may have no problem waking up on time each morning (*Day 6: Stop Waking Up Late*). But you constantly struggle with taking purposeful action (*Day 25: Stop Waiting For The Perfect Time To Act*). In that case, prioritize the habit associated with Day 25 over the one associated with Day 6.

Fourth, decide how long you'll spend on each bad

habit. You may decide to address one habit a day. Or you might opt to do one a week or even one a month. It's entirely up to you. The important thing is that you have a schedule in mind. You can change the schedule along the way, tailoring it to your personal circumstances, but have *something* in place when you start.

At the risk of being redundant, the crucial ingredient is execution. I'll provide the step-by-step plans for over-coming the 30 bad habits profiled in this book. But it's up to you to apply them. The value you receive from this book will be directly linked to the action you take. If you merely shelve this book after reading it, you won't experience the positive changes you seek. However, if you apply the advice in each chapter, I'm confident you'll be astounded by the results and inspired to continue seeking transformative change in your life.

Without further ado, let's roll up our sleeves and get started.

Day 1

~

Stop Letting Clutter Accumulate In Your Life

MOST OF US accumulate clutter in our lives. We do so for a variety of reasons.

For example, we keep gifts we don't need because we feel guilty about discarding them. We attach sentimental value to items and loathe getting rid of them because we feel emotionally connected to them. Some of us collect things in abundance (for example, we stock up on haircare products or cookbooks), convinced we'll use them eventually. Others accumulate stuff they aspire to use one day (for example, office supplies, fishing rods, and clothes), but never get around to doing so.

If you're like me, you sometimes allow your workspace to become cluttered with notepads, mail, and miscellaneous paperwork.

Whatever the reason is for the clutter, it's important to recognize its psychological effect on us. It's worth understanding how its presence prevents us from getting things done. Whether you're at home or at your workplace, clutter can ruin your productivity.

How This Bad Habit Hurts Your Productivity

CLUTTER DISTRACTS US. THE MORE "STUFF" present in our visual field, the more difficult it is for us to concentrate. In 2011, the *Journal of Neuroscience* published a study showing that increasing the number of visual stimuli *decreased* subjects' "attentional modulation" (their ability to pay attention).[1]

You know this from experience. Perhaps you intended to perform tasks around your home, but got distracted by the junk accumulating in your garage. Maybe you planned to complete an important project at work, but couldn't focus because your desk was in disarray.

The chaos of clutter hobbles our productivity because it's a constant nag on our limited attentional resources. Worse, it happens at a subliminal level. It's not always clear that the unnecessary "stuff" that's invaded your home or office is preventing you from getting things done.

The good news is that decluttering your life is a simple process. It requires diligence and resolve, but anyone can do it successfully.

Action Steps

1. Make a list of trouble areas. At home, note specific rooms, or areas of rooms, that attract clutter. At your workplace, note specific areas of your office or desk where clutter chaos reigns.

Then, address one room or area at a time. This breaks down the decluttering effort into manageable tasks so it'll seem less overwhelming.

2. Make three categories: keep, discard, and store. Then, create guidelines that determine which items will be thusly categorized. For example, you might decide to **keep** any item you intend to use during the next five days. You may decide to **discard** any item you haven't used in the last three months (for example, a shirt or blouse you've haven't worn all year). You might decide to **store** any item for which you have a specific use down the road (for example, seasonal bedding). These guidelines will streamline the decluttering process, simplifying tough decisions.

3. Assign each item in each trouble area to one of the three categories. You can do this by sticking Post-It notes on items. Or place them in boxes, each labeled with one of the three categories.

4. To prevent clutter from accumulating in the future, assign a place for every item that enters your home. You'll be less inclined to allow "stuff" to gather on your kitchen counter, workstation, family room coffee table, or inside a closet.

5. Perform a weekly purge. Once a week, inspect the trouble areas you identified in Action Step

#1. Assign every item you find to one of the three categories: keep, discard, or store. A weekly purge should only take 10 to 15 minutes. The upside is that it'll help you to stay on top of potential clutter, keeping your home and office neat and organized.

6. Develop a habit for putting things away *immediately* after using them. For example, if you use a broom to sweep your porch, store it in its place rather than allowing it to rest against a wall. If you use a stapler, bottle opener, or rubber stamp, return it to its drawer rather than leaving it on your desk or countertop.

7. Resist the impulse to buy things you don't need. We've all done it. We see an item at a store or on Amazon and think to ourselves, "*I could really use that.*" We buy it, and then never use it. Unfortunately, the item sticks around because we don't want to get rid of it without first getting our money's worth from it. This is a common cause of clutter. Resist the compulsion to buy unnecessary things to prevent future clutter from gaining a foothold in your life.

[1] https://www.ncbi.nlm.nih.gov/pubmed/21228167

Day 2

~

Stop Being Receptive To Others' Negativity

NEGATIVITY IS LIKE AN AIRBORNE VIRUS. And it has a high infection rate. If you repeatedly come within close proximity to someone afflicted with the condition, there's a good chance you'll catch it, too.

And here's the worst part: once you catch it, it's difficult to get rid of. Negativity lingers and festers. It causes harm by breaking down your resolve. Until you purge it from your system, it'll invade your thoughts, legitimize your inner critic, and slowly strip away your happiness.

It's impossible to avoid negativity entirely. Whether we're at home or at our workplaces, we're going to be exposed to people who are habitually negative. You know the type… they're chronically unhappy, constantly complaining, and continually stressed about potential disaster. They backbite and gossip, lie and tell secrets, and are quick to condemn. They're deceitful, selfish, envious, and overly sensitive to constructive feedback.

Their habitual pessimism and cynicism are highly contagious. If you catch these maladies, you'll find it's almost impossible to work productively over the long run.

How This Bad Habit Hurts Your Productivity

FIRST, prolonged negativity is exhausting. It encourages harmful emotions that make you feel fatigued and lethargic. This lack of energy, in turn, creates internal resistance that counters your inclination to take action.

Second, negativity puts you in a foul mood. Think of someone you know who's always negative. Does he or she ever seem happy or content? Probably not. On the contrary, this person likely has a perpetually gloomy outlook, is constantly frustrated, and usually in a bad frame of mind. When was the last time you were productive when feeling this way?

Third, there's evidence that harboring negative thoughts can adversely affect how we perceive, learn, and reason.[1] This alone should give us pause and motivate us to consider how receptive we are to others' negativity.

Exposure to negative people is unavoidable. The key is how you interact with them. You can't change them, so don't try. Instead, focus on inoculating yourself from their sullen, dismal outlook.

Action Steps

1. Identify negative people in your life. Do so

regarding those at your workplace as well as those with whom you're socially involved.

2. Limit the time you spend with negative family members. This advice may seem harsh. Most of us are naturally inclined to tolerate our families regardless of how abrasive, insulting, and emotionally abusive they are. But if a family member's constant cynicism or pessimism is having a corrosive effect on your outlook, it's time to say goodbye. If you feel comfortable doing so, explain to the person why you intend to pull back. Give him or her the opportunity to change. After all, he or she is family.

3. Limit the time you spend with negative friends and acquaintances. Just because you've been friends with a negative person for years doesn't mean you're obligated to continue being so. Surround yourself with people who are positive, optimistic, and supportive.

4. Limit the time you spend with negative coworkers. Because you're working alongside these people, it's infeasible to avoid them altogether. But you *can* dictate the rules concerning how you interact with them. For example, if a coworker has a penchant for complaining, stop him when he begins to do so. Let him know that you're busy. Then ask him,

"Is there anything else I can help you with?" This
approach conveys your willingness to lend a
hand with business-related matters. But you
don't have time for his negativity.

5. Refrain from correcting negative people. If a
   family member gossips about another family
   member, and you know the gossip is untrue, let
   it go. If a friend makes a provably false
   assertion in an attempt to start an argument
   with you, don't engage. If a coworker makes a
   complaint you feel is unjustified, reply with a
   simple "Huh. Is that so?" and remove yourself
   from the conversation.

6. Avoid all drama. Most drama is caused by
   pernicious, argumentative, and bored
   individuals. They relish the opportunity to
   make waves. The havoc they create in the
   process is its own reward. No good can come
   from getting involved. Avoid drama like the
   plague. Don't pick a side. Don't attack or
   defend. Don't engage at all. Simply walk away.

7. Celebrate the successes experienced by negative
   people. Your positivity will short circuit their
   inclination to complain, gossip, or criticize. But
   keep it brief. If a negative coworker receives a
   promotion, smile and congratulate him or her,
   and move on. If a negative friend mentions that
   he just became engaged, say "That's terrific!

Congratulations!" and leave it at that. If given the opportunity, habitually-pessimistic people will show you the negativity of any joyful circumstance.

[1] https://www.ncbi.nlm.nih.gov/pubmed/2303569

∼

Stop Allowing Negative Self-Talk To Kill Your Momentum

EACH OF US has an inner critic. It sits in the background criticizing us, whispering that we're neither smart enough nor good enough. It tries to convince us that our decisions and actions are certain to result in catastrophe.

This is negative self-talk. It can have a debilitating effect on our productivity.

It manifests in many forms. For example, perfectionism is oftentimes an expression of negative self-talk. Perfectionists believe that anything less than perfect is a failure, an outlook that prevents them from taking action.

Catastrophizing is another sign of negative self-talk. A person who catastrophizes believes disaster is imminent. Like the perfectionist, he or she is disinclined to take action since doing so is likely (at least in his or her mind) to produce dreadful results.

Polarizing is also evidence of our inner critics at work. This is a tendency to see everything as black or white. There is no middle ground. An individual sees himself or herself as either smart or dumb, attractive or ugly, successful or hopeless, right or wrong.

Negative self-talk, given voice by our inner critics, can be paralyzing - at home and at our workplaces.

How This Bad Habit Hurts Your Productivity

SELF-CRITICISM IS like a bad friend who wishes you to fail. It watches for the smallest ember of doubt and stokes it until it's ablaze. It looks for ways to dampen your positive attitude until you become convinced that you're ineffectual.

At that point, every task becomes a huge undertaking darkened by a cloud of potential failure. Every responsibility promises disaster and thereby validation of your inner critic's assertions.

It's difficult to work productively when we have this perspective about ourselves and our abilities. In the worst cases, where negative self-talk is allowed to run rampant, it's almost *impossible* to work. We become paralyzed with doubt. We're powerless to act for fear of proving that our inner critics' claims are correct.

The good news is, you can tame your inner critic and silence negative self-talk. All it takes is developing a few simple habits. Once you do so, you'll find it much easier to make decisions and take purposeful action in every area of your life.

Action Steps

1. Learn to recognize the signs of self-criticism. Focus on what your inner voice is saying about you and your abilities. Note how its recrimination makes you feel. It may at first be difficult to connect your inner critic with the negative feelings you have toward yourself. That's common. Many people have struggled with self-criticism for so long that the signs are hidden in plain sight. Pay attention to your *automatic* responses to new events, thoughts, and other stimuli. Are your thoughts positive or negative?

2. Remind yourself that your inner critic's claims are merely assertions. Nothing more. If you scrutinize them, you'll find they're indefensible. Confront assertions head-on and ask for evidence. For example, suppose you plan to attend a social event, and your inner critic claims no one will like you. Challenge the assertion by asking for proof. If you have friends, the claim is demonstrably false. Don't be afraid to call your inner critic a liar.

3. Reframe negative thoughts so they're impartial and unprejudiced. Make them neutral. For example, suppose you're confronted with an unfamiliar task. Your inner critic might immediately claim, "*You don't possess the necessary knowledge or skills.*" Reframe this claim by saying to yourself, "*It'll be a challenge.*"

4. Write down every expression of self-criticism. Keep it in a small journal, either online (e.g. using Evernote) or in a physical notebook (e.g. a Moleskine planner). The purpose of doing so is to gather evidence of your inner critic's chicanery. You'll be able to refer to it down the road and easily recognize how little substance the claims have.

5. Enlist an internal ally. In *Day 2*, we talked about replacing toxic people in your life with those who are positive and optimistic. Use this same approach to silence your inner critic. Cultivate an inner voice that not only counters the false claims, but drowns them out by highlighting your positive attributes. Using our "social event" example from earlier, your internal ally would remind you that you have friends because you're honest, reliable, and fun to be around.

6. Adopt a growth mindset. This mindset recognizes that there's always room for improvement. We're constantly learning, getting smarter, and adding to our abilities. That being the case, we're able to take on bigger responsibilities and experience greater achievements than we have in the past. When you accept the fact that you're capable of achieving things today that you weren't capable

of achieving yesterday, negative self-talk will
have less power over you.

Day 4

~

Stop Overlooking Weekly Reviews

CONDUCTING weekly reviews gives us an opportunity to evaluate our productivity over the past seven days. They give us a chance to assess how effective we were. Did we complete everything we set out to accomplish? Or do important to-do items remain unfinished? If the latter is the case, why? Further, how should we prioritize them for the coming week?

Many people feel that reviewing their performance each week is a waste of time. They believe they're effective at work and at home, and that spending time each week to examine their effectiveness would therefore be meaningless.

Others ignore weekly reviews because they're unsure how to conduct them. They recognize the value in appraising their weekly performance, but are unfamiliar with the steps involved with doing so.

In the Action Steps below, I'll show you how to conduct a simple weekly review. But first, let's consider how their omission is harming your productivity.

How This Bad Habit Hurts Your Productivity

WE LEAD BUSY LIVES, both at work and at home. It some-times seems as if we're saddled with more tasks, chores, and obligations than we have time to complete them. It's no wonder we feel frazzled and exhausted at the end of the week. It's a Herculean effort just to make it to the weekend, and even then, we have responsibilities that require our attention.

Without conducting weekly reviews, it's difficult to identify problems that are hobbling your productivity. For example, did you take on more responsibilities last week than you should have given your available time? Did you agree to meetings at work or get-togethers with friends that ended up infringing upon other obligations? Did you create a mile-long to-do list, ultimately setting yourself up for failure and disappointment? Did you fall behind on paper-work, bills, and email, and ignore important relationships because you were handling crises that could have been avoided with better planning?

None of us is perfect in how we work. There is *always* room for improvement. When we improve our approach to work, both at home and at the office, we feel more orga-nized and in control. We feel more empowered. We also free up time to pursue activities that are important to us.

That's the value in conducting weekly reviews. They show us how to optimize our processes, helping us to get more work done in less time, and enjoy ourselves more in the process.

Action Steps

1. Commit 30 minutes to each review session. No more. No less. Performing weekly reviews is daunting to many people because they expect the practice to require hours. In truth, you should be able to complete it in 30 minutes.

2. Put the weekly review sessions on your calendar. This will train your mind to consider it an action item, and you'll be less likely to disregard it. Choose a day and time that works for you and be consistent. For example, I perform my weekly reviews on Sunday evenings at 7:00 p.m.

3. Review tasks, chores, and projects that lingered from the past week. Ponder the reasons. For example, did you neglect to set aside sufficient time for them? Were you wrangled into unrelated projects and activities that reduced your availability? Did you say yes to people to whom you should have said no? Did you procrastinate, were you unfocused, or were you repeatedly distracted by social media? Once you know the reasons that select tasks, chores, and projects lingered from the *past* week, you can plan how you'll avoid such circumstances during the *coming* week.

4. Ask yourself what went *well* last week. What did

you do that worked for you? For example, did you resist the temptation to say yes to people, focusing instead on your own to-do list? Did you install a site blocker in your browser to prevent yourself from being distracted by Youtube, Facebook, and Instagram? Did you wake up earlier each morning, giving yourself an opportunity to work in quietude while your family slept? If a tactic worked for you last week, it should work for you in the coming week.

5. Clean your email inbox. Email is a source of stress for many of us. It accumulates quickly and can become overwhelming without constant attention. During your weekly review, spend 10 minutes addressing lingering emails. You may be tempted to reply to each one. Resist that temptation. Many emails require no response. Place those that *do* into a special folder within your email program (I use Gmail, and creating folders is simple). Archive or delete the rest.

6. Plan the coming week on your calendar. What do you need to accomplish? Which tasks and projects are high-priority items and which can be relegated to a lower-priority to-do list? During this planning stage, use the intel gleaned during Action Step #3 to optimize each day.

For example, if you discovered that you set aside insufficient time to complete important tasks last week, dedicate larger time chunks for those tasks during the coming week.

Stop Neglecting To Unplug For Extended Periods

"I DON'T HAVE time to take a vacation!"

Does that sound familiar? We love the *idea* of taking time off. Just the thought of relaxing for a week, separated from the stresses of our jobs and the busyness of our lives, causes us to sigh with relief. But when the time comes to actually *take* a vacation, we hesitate. We think about the potential consequences of unplugging for an extended period. Will our work and careers suffer? Is taking time off feasible given our home and social responsibilities?

In the U.S., people seem unwilling to take long breaks. Studies show that Americans regularly forego using their vacation days, preferring instead to spend that time at their jobs.[1] But this isn't a geographic problem; it's a *human* problem. Data compiled by the UK's Office of National Statistics show that English workers are just as reluctant to take holiday time.[2]

Neglecting to unplug carries significant downsides. Not only is it detrimental to our general health and happiness, but it can ruin our productivity over time.

How This Bad Habit Hurts Your Productivity

BUSYNESS, at home, at the office, or in our social lives, causes mental fatigue. Constantly making decisions chips away at our cognitive resources, leaving us feeling stressed, irritable, apathetic, and emotionally exhausted. If this circumstance persists, it'll eventually impact our ability to work efficiently.

We'll find it increasingly difficult to focus. We'll lose our motivation to tackle important tasks, betraying our convictions to work in a manner consistent with our high standards. Many of us silently congratulate ourselves for our perseverance and work ethic, even while our workaholic ways threaten to wreak havoc on our productivity.

The stresses of your normal day may seem manageable. But they take a cognitive toll over time. Worse, that toll may be all but invisible, even as it consistently erodes your performance.

The solution is to unplug. Take an extended break. Doing so may seem impractical given your responsibilities and obligations, both at home and at work. But you'll find that taking time off will make you feel happier, relaxed and refreshed, and enthusiastic, all of which will boost your productivity when you return.

Not sure how to make it happen? Read on.

Action Steps

1. Pick a date. Don't wait until your job, your
    home life, and your social life align perfectly.
    They won't. There will always be a project,
    activity, or task that needs your attention. If you
    wait for a clear window to magically appear on
    your calendar, you'll never break free. Force the
    issue by scheduling time off, and alerting others
    of your plans.

2. Make a list of every meeting, project, and task,
    both at home and at work, that needs your
    attention. Schedule time blocks on your
    calendar to address these items in the weeks
    leading up to your vacation. People often refuse
    to take time off because they feel doing so
    forces them to abandon important to-do items.
    Handle such items ahead of time, even if it
    means devoting extra time to them each day.
    Work hard to clear the space on your calendar.

3. Commit to *not* working during your vacation.
    It's tempting to take your laptop with you,
    rationalizing that you'll spend just a few
    minutes each day returning emails and
    completing small tasks. But the amount of time
    you spend working isn't the issue. The *true* issue
    is that working during your vacation maintains
    the connection to your normal busyness. The
    point of taking time off is to temporarily *sever*
    this connection.

4. Schedule time off around company holidays.

For example, suppose your workplace will be closed next Monday. Plan to take off the preceding Friday as well as the following Tuesday and Wednesday. Long weekends (Saturday, Sunday, and Monday) tend to slow the pace of activity in most offices. Take advantage of this fact. Unplug when your presence will be less critical.

5. If you're hesitant to ask your employer for time off, there are tactics you can use to smooth the process. First, avoid requesting time off during your company's peak time of year. Second, send the request via email so you'll have documentation. Third, give as much advance notice as possible. (Following Action Step #1 will help. After all, the longer you wait to pick a date, the shorter notice you'll be forced to give your employer. Consequently, there's a greater likelihood your request will be denied.) Fourth, ask your boss when the best time would be for you to take a vacation. Put the ball in his or her court. If you're working on a project, you might suggest the period immediately following its completion. Fifth, present a plan regarding how your workload will be divvied among your coworkers in your absence. (Negotiate the details with your coworkers before you approach your boss with your vacation request.)

6. Plan a staycation. Not every vacation needs to

involve heavy traveling and luxurious destinations. Remember, the point is to sever the connection between you and your normally frenetic routine. You can accomplish this goal at home, as long as you commit to not working. The upside is that you'll save money, you'll already know how to get around town, and you'll enjoy the personal comforts to which you're accustomed. You'll also avoid the inevitable irritations that accompany traveling (e.g. lost luggage, screaming babies on planes, etc.).

[1] https://projecttimeoff.com/reports/state-of-american-vacation-2018/

[2] https://www.consultancy.uk/news/13652/overworked-britons-wasted-163-million-annual-leave-days-in-2016

Day 6

~

Stop Waking Up Late

WHAT DO Apple CEO Tim Cook, business magnate Sir Richard Branson, Starbucks CEO Howard Schultz, and *Dilbert* creator Scott Adams all have in common?

If you thought to yourself, "They're all highly successful and extremely effective," you'd be right. But there's another trait that connects them: they're early risers. And in interviews, they attribute much of their daily success to this habit.

Think about the last time you awoke late in the morning. Perhaps you kept hitting the snooze button on your phone or clock. Maybe you decided to forego an alarm altogether. How did you feel when you finally climbed out of bed? Energetic or tired? Alert or groggy? Purposeful or aimless? If you're like me, you probably felt like the latter in each case. Getting up later than intended has a draining effect.

It's not that being an early riser alone makes you more productive. In fact, many people work more effectively waking up at 9:00 a.m. than 5:00 a.m. The most important factors are intention and consistency. Waking up each morning *when you intend to do so*, and doing it *regularly*, make you more effective. At least, that's what Harvard researchers found when they studied students' academic performance and compared it to the students' sleep habits. [1] Sleep regularity had a notable impact on performance.

If you habitually wake up later than you intend to, you're hampering your productivity.

How This Bad Habit Hurts Your Productivity

FIRST, people who wake up later than they intend often suffer from poor sleep quality. The irregularity of their sleep hours affects their internal clock (i.e. their circadian rhythm), which prevents them from enjoying restful slumber.

For example, have you ever stayed up late to binge-watch your favorite show on Netflix, and consequently woken up late the next morning? Did you feel woozy and disoriented? That's understandable given that you threw off your sleep/wake cycle. It's difficult to be productive when you disrupt your circadian rhythm. The disruption causes your brain to send the wrong signals to your body (e.g. releasing melatonin at the wrong time).

Second, waking up late due to irregular sleep habits encourages feelings of lethargy. Getting out of bed later than planned siphons our enthusiasm about our day. We feel listless and without purpose. We may even experience anxiety because a part of our day has unintentionally slipped through our fingers. Worse, it might be impossible to salvage our most productive hours.

If you're currently struggling with this issue, you *can* turn things around. It's just a matter of implementing a few simple habits that'll ensure you wake up on time each morning.

Action Steps

1. Go to bed at the same time each evening. Resist the temptation to binge-watch Netflix. Avoid becoming entangled in a Facebook thread. Steer clear of Youtube, where it's common to lose track of time while watching product reviews, gaming videos, and comedy skits. Choose a time to go to bed and stick to it. Be consistent.

2. Commit to waking up at the same time each morning. Avoid sleeping in, even on the weekends. It's more important to maintain your body's circadian rhythm than take advantage of extra time you might have on select mornings.

3. Avoid drinking alcohol before going to bed. Many people believe alcohol to be a sleep aid. Researchers *have* associated it with delta waves,

which are typically seen during deep stage 3 of non-rapid eye movement sleep.[2] But alcohol does more harm than good when it comes to sleep *quality*. While it's connected to delta waves, it's also connected to alpha waves. These latter waves are seen during wakeful relaxation. They're supposed to *decline* as we enter deep sleep. Ultimately, alcohol prevents us from enjoying deep, restful sleep, and makes it more difficult to wake up on time in the morning.

4. Place your phone or alarm clock several feet away from your bed. If it's sitting on your nightstand within reach, you may be tempted to turn it off (or hit snooze) and go back to sleep. Placing it beyond your easy reach will force you to get out of bed to turn it off. Once you're out of bed, you'll find it much easier to start your day.

5. Know what you're going to do upon waking each morning. Will you go to the gym immediately after getting out of bed? Will you retreat to your home office and start responding to emails? Do you have a morning routine in place, one that includes journaling, meditation, and reading while enjoying a cup of coffee? Such plans represent *reasons* for waking up on time. They'll compel you to get out of bed when you're tempted to remain under the covers.

[1] https://www.nature.com/articles/s41598-017-03171-4

[2]
https://www.ncbi.nlm.nih.gov/pmc/articles/PMC582125
9/

Day 7

~

Stop Responding Immediately To Email, Texts, And Voicemails

WE LIVE in an age where quick responses to email, texts, voicemails, and even messages on Facebook are applauded. Conversely, slow responses are given the side eye; they're met with disapproval. Everyone knows this intuitively, creating a societal expectation for instant reachability. Consequently, many of us try to respond to messages as quickly as possible lest our friends, family members, or bosses think ill of us.

But there's a downside to maintaining this habit: it quashes our productivity. The more inclined we are to respond instantly to others' emails, texts, and voicemails, the less able we are to work in an efficient manner.

How This Bad Habit Hurts Your Productivity

THE BIGGEST PROBLEM with replying immediately to others' messages is that each time we do so constitutes an interruption. Such interruptions may seem innocuous because they tend to be short in duration, but they can destroy our ability to focus. Researchers have found that it takes our brains more than 20 minutes to get back on track following an interruption.[1]

That's a lot of wasted time. If you respond to texts and emails several times each hour, you can imagine why it's so difficult to get things done.

A second problem is that quick responses to messages create an expectation in those who have reached out to you. Once you respond immediately to a person's texts and emails, there's a subtle presumption that you'll continue doing so down the road. The pressure may be unspoken, but it's present nevertheless. Indeed, failure to respond quickly to the individual may elicit an emotional response. Your instant reachability, initially offered in a spirit of pleasantness, is now considered obligatory by him or her.

Trying to satisfy these unjustified expectations is a recipe for frustration. Moreover, doing so can severely impair your ability to work productively.

If you've developed a habit of immediately responding to others' messages, it's time to make a healthy change. Here's how to reclaim your time and modify others' expectations regarding your reachability in the process.

Action Steps

1. Forget about etiquette. The first step in making any type of positive change in your life is

recognizing that others' expectations are less important than your wellbeing and happiness. Don't worry that your friends will think you're being rude if you fail to immediately reply to their texts. Don't concern yourself with the fear that your coworkers will consider you to be impolite if you fail to instantaneously respond to their emails. Etiquette "rules" vary from person to person. Commit to meeting standards that make sense to *you*, even if they differ from *others'* standards.

2. Check email twice per day. Pick two times - for example, 11:00 a.m. and 5:00 p.m. - and stick to them. Resist the temptation to check and respond to emails outside those windows. Once upon a time, checking and replying to emails meant logging in to our email programs on our computers. That required us to be at our desks or carry around a laptop, both useful impediments in this regard. These days, with our phones within reach at all times, we can - and often do - check and reply to emails during every waking moment. But doing so is a bad idea for the reasons noted above.

3. Respond to texts twice per day. Apply the same protocol we used for email (see above). Pick two times and stick to them. In my opinion, it's advantageous to check and reply to texts at the same times you check and reply to emails. It's a

similar activity, so it's sensible to batch them. Doing so saves time. For example, you may notice emails and texts that were sent by the same person. There's no need to respond to all of them. Send a single email or text in response. Replying to texts only twice per day may be difficult at first. It's likely counter to what you're currently doing - replying dozens of times per day. But once you acknowledge that there's no *need* to check and reply that frequently, it'll become easier to develop the habit without anxiety.

4. The protocols described above will go a long way toward reshaping others' expectations regarding your reachability. People will eventually grow accustomed to having to wait to hear back from you. Unfortunately, some of your friends, family members, and coworkers may feel snubbed during this process. They'll convince themselves that you're treating them with disrespect by choosing to not reply immediately to their messages. Dampen their irritation by communicating your intentions ahead of time. Let your friends and family members know that you intend to check email and texts twice per day. Speak with your boss regarding whether doing so is feasible given your work-related responsibilities (mention that you'll be more focused and productive). If it is,

communicate your intentions to your
coworkers.

5. If your job demands that you check email,
   texts, and voicemails throughout the day, apply
   a GTD protocol. Touch each message only
   once, deciding immediately what to do with it.
   For example, an urgent email from your boss
   might warrant an instant response. A text from
   a coworker might require no action at all, and
   can safely be disregarded and archived. A
   voicemail from a vendor or client may require
   follow-up once you retrieve specific
   information. Schedule a callback based on
   when you'll be in possession of the information
   you need. This is a less-than-ideal situation, of
   course. But if you have no choice, using a GTD
   protocol will streamline the interruptions.

[1] https://www.ics.uci.edu/~gmark/chi08-mark.pdf

~

Stop Allowing Yourself To Be Easily Distracted

DISTRACTIONS ARE among the worst productivity killers for three reasons. First, they're often insidious. They're subtle to the point of escaping our notice, either because of exposure or habit. For example, a ringing phone seems routine and harmless, but draws our attention as effectively as a car accident.

Second, distractions prey upon our desire to avoid work. How many times have you found yourself visiting Facebook, Youtube, and news websites while you were supposed to be working? It's almost as if the brain actively *looks* for stimuli to distract it.

Third, once we're distracted from our work, it's difficult to get back on track. We lose momentum. In some cases, we become inclined to stop working altogether, surrendering ourselves entirely to the distraction.

Needless to say, this can cripple your productivity.

How This Bad Habit Hurts Your Productivity

DISTRACTIONS HURT your productivity in five important ways. First, they weaken your focus. When you're doing "deep work," the type of work that requires all of your attentional resources, a single distraction can disrupt your flow. Once your concentration is broken, it's difficult to regain it.

Second, distractions can harm the quality of your work. It's easier to produce high-quality output when you work without interruption. When you become distracted, the overall quality of your product is likely to suffer. You're also likely to require more time to complete tasks and become more prone to making mistakes along the way.

Third, distractions reduce your patience. The more distracted you are, the more frustrated you're likely to become as your productivity declines. This circumstance, if allowed to persist, can become irksome to the point that you find yourself less accommodating to adverse conditions. You start snapping at coworkers, ignoring your friends, and berating yourself for deficits you'd otherwise forgive.

Fourth, distractions can cause important items to fall through the cracks. Have you ever been distracted while working on a task or project only to forget to return to it later? We may chalk up such incidents as evidence of forgetfulness, as if we lacked the power to effect a different outcome. In truth, however, the issue is that we were distracted, a circumstance that's arguably under our control.

Fifth, distractions make us less attentive. Although

many people claim to be effective multitaskers, the brain doesn't address multiple tasks at once. It switches between them. The greater the number of tasks we try to address at once, the less attention we can devote to each of them. Our attentiveness declines as our brains attempt to process each stimulus.

The good news is, learning to ignore distractions is simple. Fair warning: it'll take time and you'll need to adopt a few new practices to counteract the distraction habit. The upside is, the results will pay dividends for years to come.

Action Steps

1. Turn off your phone while you work. That way, you can avoid the distracting chirps and beeps caused by incoming texts, calls, and notifications.

2. Close every unnecessary browser tab. Bookmark pages so you can read them later. If you leave the tabs open, you'll be tempted to read them now instead of working. Remember, the brain looks for things to distract it from hard work.

3. Learn to recognize the telltale signs of distraction. For example, is your mind wandering from the task at hand? Are you making careless mistakes? Are you feeling an

urge to do something unrelated to the work in front of you? If the answer is yes, you're probably distracted.

4. The moment you feel yourself becoming distracted, stop what you're doing. Close your eyes, take a deep breath, and remind yourself of the reasons you're doing whatever you're doing. For example, if you're cleaning your home, you might remind yourself that you'll be hosting a party this evening. If you're studying, remind yourself that you have an important exam tomorrow. If you're examining a report for your job, remind yourself that you're giving a presentation later that week and need to be familiar with the material.

5. Do activities that'll improve your ability to focus. For example, read long-form articles that require your attention for true comprehension. Practice your listening skills by watching TED Talk videos. Meditate, forcing your mind to remain quiet and still for five to ten minutes at a time. Your ability to concentrate is like a muscle. The more you exercise it, the stronger it'll become and the better equipped you'll be to ignore distractions.

6. Ask your family members and coworkers to allow you to work uninterrupted during specific blocks of time. Let them know that you'll be available for them before and after these time

blocks. This will help to prevent distractions before they occur. Good preparation increases the odds of success. As Abraham Lincoln once said, *"Give me six hours to chop down a tree and I will spend the first four sharpening the axe."*

Day 9

~

Stop Being Emotionally Dependent On Others

EMOTIONAL DEPENDENCY IS when our emotional state is dictated by another person. Our happiness depends on what this individual says or does. We feel as if we always want to be near him or her, and obsess over losing his or her favor. Deep down, we might even feel as if we're not "good enough" to share a connection with this person. Of course, that feeling exacerbates the obsession. Ultimately, we feel helpless toward fulfilling our own needs.

Emotional dependency is typically discussed in the context of romantic relationships. But it can be just as big a problem among friends, neighbors, family members, and coworkers. In some cases, interaction with complete *strangers* can impact our emotions to the point that we feel dejected and distressed.

As you can imagine, this problem can have a debilitating effect on your ability to get things done.

How This Bad Habit Hurts Your Productivity

ONE OF THE symptoms of emotional dependency is anxiety. It stems from a constant need for validation from the person upon whom you're emotionally dependent. Anxiety impedes productivity. It's difficult to focus when you're overcome with fear and insecurity. And if you're unable to focus, your performance and quality of work will suffer.

Another symptom of emotional dependency is anger when the individual fails to respond in the way we expect. We infer an implicit rejection in his or her response, even if no such rejection is implied or intended. Anger is simultaneously distracting and exhausting. It's almost impossible to concentrate when we're aggravated. Worse, persistent aggravation can drain our energy and willpower, leaving us with scant resources to work productively.

When we're emotionally dependent on someone, we become fixated on that individual. In the process, we allow the inevitable negative feelings that arise from our obsession over that relationship to take control of our minds. And that, in turn, negatively affects our behavior.

Below, you'll find several tips that'll help you to break the emotional dependency you might feel toward others. If you incorporate them into your day, you'll experience a growing sense of emotional self-reliance. You'll gradually become able to meet your own emotional needs, freeing up your attentional resources to devote toward important work.

Action Steps

1. Create something for yourself. Write a private journal. Concoct a delicious sauce or marinade, and keep the recipe to yourself. If you play the guitar, write a song and share it with no one. The purpose of this activity is to give yourself opportunities to revel in your own creativity. External validation is unnecessary.

2. Look for ways to enjoy "alone" time. Seek activities that exclude the person upon whom you're emotionally dependent. For example, grab a book and visit a local Starbucks. Visit a park during low-traffic hours and enjoy the solitude. Take a walk by yourself. These activities will reinforce the idea that you don't need to depend on anyone else for your happiness.

3. Learn a new skill. For example, learn to draw, play guitar, or use Photoshop. Learn how to defend yourself, how to dance, or how to cook a specific type of cuisine. Learn a new language, how to give a speech, or how to perform CPR. Learning new things makes us more confident. It's evidence of self-efficacy. This confidence, which grows as you witness the broadening of your abilities, will counter the emotional dependence you feel toward others.

4. Improve yourself. Seek opportunities for personal development. For example, learn how to take action (stop procrastinating), listen

actively, or get up earlier in the morning. Learn how to manage stress, make better decisions, and be more resilient in the face of adversity. As with learning new skills, improving ourselves strengthens our *belief* in ourselves. We become more inclined to see ourselves as the authors of our own success. Along the way, we become less dependent on other people for our happiness.

5. Accept responsibility for your emotional well-being. For example, if you feel angry, recognize that your anger stems from your own perspective rather than something done to you by another person. If you feel lonely, acknowledge that your loneliness arises from your thoughts and expectations rather than someone else's actions. If you feel anxious, admit to yourself that your anxiety is internally driven rather than caused by others.

   Admittedly, taking responsibility for your emotional state is easier said than done. But it's doable if you take small steps. Focus on a single emotion that challenges you on a regular basis. For example, suppose you feel constantly exasperated by a friend's actions. The next time you feel this way, remind yourself that you control your responses. To that end, you control whether you experience exasperation.

6. Make decisions for yourself without seeking approval from others. For example, suppose you

aspire to write a novel. Refrain from asking your spouse, friends, and family members for their opinions regarding your decision. Instead, simply decide to do it and move forward. This exercise trains your mind to put less stock in others' validation of your decisions. Instead, you'll become more emotionally self-reliant. Making decisions without approval may be difficult at first if you're unaccustomed to doing so. But the more often you do it, the easier it'll become.

Day 10

~

Stop Letting Money Stress Consume You

To start, we're not always to blame for out-of-control finances. Circumstances beyond our influence often conspire to derail our financial goals and create money stress. For example, a single medical emergency can wipe out months - even years - of consistent savings.

Having said that, many people struggle with money issues that stem directly from their choices. For example, they live beyond their means. They neglect to save for a rainy day. They fail to learn how to properly manage money and credit as they accumulate more possessions. I speak from experience; I'm guilty of having committed each of these sins in the past.

I can genuinely say, there's no stress like money stress. When you're worried about unpaid utility bills, voluminous credit card balances, and an empty savings account, it's nearly impossible to focus and be productive.

If you're struggling with financial pressure, you're not alone. According to a 2017 report released by Bank of America, 53% of U.S. workers are so stressed about money that it's negatively affecting their job performance.[1]

Let's take a look at the reasons.

How This Bad Habit Hurts Your Productivity

WHEN YOUR FINANCES are out of control, it's natural to experience anxiety. Uncertainty about the future causes distress, which can consume your attention. That's why it's so hard to focus when you're concerned about how you'll make ends meet. Financial problems are a major stressor. And persistent stress is a significant impediment to productivity.

Money problems can also affect your sleep quality. Have you ever lain in bed, unable to sleep due to worries that you'll be unable to pay your bills? The next morning, you might have risen out of bed feeling lethargic, mentally fatigued, and depressed. It's difficult to work, much less do so *efficiently*, when you're burdened with feelings that prevent you from enjoying good-quality sleep.

If you're in a huge financial hole, you might even experience feelings of hopelessness. This is the point at which financial pressure can impact your physical health. It's not uncommon for chronic money stress to cause migraines, gastrointestinal problems, and high blood pressure.

Because our financial state has such an enormous effect on our mental - and sometimes physical - well-being, it pays to properly manage our money. If you feel stressed because your finances are out of control, take the following steps to remedy the situation. You may be surprised by how quickly things can turn around in your favor.

Action Steps

1. Recognize there's no shame in having money problems. Nearly everyone has struggled with such problems at some point in their lives. This means everyone can relate to the predicament on a personal level. Shame does nothing but invite guilt, and neither will contribute toward a solution.

2. Take a close look at your financial picture. Money stress is largely borne of uncertainty. You may have a vague idea of your financial status, but lack the details that allow you to take purposeful action. For example, you might know your credit card balances are high, but are unsure of the precise numbers. You may know you're spending too much each month given your income, but are unsure of where the money is going. Take a hard look at your monthly inflows and outflows. Know where you stand in relation to your financial responsibilities.

3. Create a realistic budget. First, look at your monthly expenses. Second, look at the expenses that occur once every three months, six months,

and twelve months - for example, car insurance. Third, figure out how much money you bring home each month after taxes. Fourth, formulate a plan to pay off your credit card balances. Don't merely pay the minimum due each month. Fifth, institute a savings plan whereby you put away a certain amount of money each month. If you have credit card balances, keep the amount you save small. The purpose is to develop the savings habit. Devote the rest to paying off your credit cards. As you pay them off, start allocating the money earmarked for the monthly payments toward your savings.

4. If you need to increase your monthly inflow to get your financial picture in order, consider ways to make extra money in your spare time. There are countless legitimate ways to do so without special training. For example, you could drive for Uber or Lyft on the weekends. You could offer pet-sitting services through Rover.com. You could perform odd jobs for people in your city, securing gigs through TaskRabbit.com. Or you can offer services online via Fiverr.com. The point is, a "side hustle" can help you bring in more money each month. Use the extra income to pay down your credit cards or jumpstart your savings and investment plan.

5. Once you pay off your credit card balances,

automate your savings plan. Set up a plan through your bank whereby a certain amount of money is automatically transferred from your checking account into your savings account. This transfer will occur on a day you select (e.g. the seventh of each month).

6. Commit to saving a specific amount of money (e.g. $10,000). These savings will constitute your emergency fund. This is the money you'll dip into when you need to pay for unanticipated expenses (e.g. car repairs, replacement water heater, etc.). Once you reach your determined dollar amount, modify the automatic savings plan we created in Action Step #5. Rather than transferring money from your checking account to your savings account (i.e. your emergency fund), begin transferring funds into an investment account. I recommend mutual funds because they're simple and offer instant diversification.

[1]
http://benefitplans.baml.com/publish/content/application/pdf/GWMOL/2017WorkplaceBenefitsReport_ARKRNPFQ.pdf

Day 11

~

Stop Spending Time With Toxic People

TOXIC PEOPLE WILL MAKE you feel terrible about yourself and the world around you. They're negative and more likely to criticize than praise. They're prone to lying and manipulation, and consumed with thoughts of revenge against those they perceived as having wronged them in some way.

Other habits exhibited by toxic people are subtler, but just as offensive. They tend to be self-absorbed, routinely interrupting conversations to direct attention toward themselves. They attract drama, usually in a bid for validation of their own moral or ethical superiority. They're instantly judgmental of others, pointing out traits they consider to be character deficits.

We talked briefly about negative people in *Day 2*. There, we discussed these individuals in the context of their general negativity. Here, we'll focus on truly *toxic* individuals and their machinations. If you currently spend time with such people, it's in your interest to remove them from your life. Doing so will make you happier, more confident, and ultimately more productive.

How This Bad Habit Hurts Your Productivity

ONE OF THE worst consequences of spending time with toxic people is the way you begin to feel about yourself. Criticism is contagious. It's impossible to be around these individuals for long without eventually turning the spotlight on your own perceived shortcomings. This gives your inner critic license to wreak havoc on your self-esteem and self-confidence. It's difficult to get things done when you constantly feel bad about yourself.

Spending time with people who are continuously unkind and unpleasant will sap your energy. It'll tax your motivation and willpower as these resources must be spent navigating the precarious minefield that is the toxic person's domain. Recall when you last spent time with someone who disparaged everyone and everything around him or her. Wasn't it draining? Didn't you feel exhausted after the experience? Perhaps you even felt anxious and stressed out. These are some of the effects of hanging around toxic people. It's easy to see how doing so can hobble your productivity.

Here's how to cut toxic people from your life and spend the resources they consume on building healthy relationships that inspire you.

Action Steps

1. The most important step is putting yourself first. If you're in a toxic relationship, it's easy to become accustomed to being a doormat. Your role is to cater to the other person's foul outlook, listening to his vitriol and offering support for his endless string of crises. Putting yourself first is an act of self-compassion. It's a claim to your right to live a life that makes you happy. To that end, it's a declaration that you're unwilling to let a toxic person influence your outlook or harm your mental and emotional well-being.

2. Consider how you'll be positively affected by removing toxic people from your life. How will doing so impact your family life? How about your social life? How will it affect your career? How will cutting out toxic people impact your *other* relationships? (It'll likely allow them to flourish.) Ultimately, will cutting out toxic people make you happier, more positive, and more self-assured? (The answer will be "yes" to all three.) The purpose of this step is to give you the impetus to act. Once you're keenly aware of the benefits you'll enjoy, you'll have the motivation - and even urgency - to move forward.

3. Be proactive in severing toxic relationships. It's tempting to be standoffish to toxic people, hoping they'll get the hint and seek someone

else to use as their doormat. But this passive approach is just as likely to elicit anger and demands for an explanation. It's better to explain upfront why you're severing the connection. Sit down with the toxic individual and describe why you're ending the relationship. Highlight how their behavior impacts you. Don't assert that their behavior is wrongheaded or dishonorable. Rather, simply focus on how it affects you. For example, you might say, *"You criticize me a lot. Each time you do so, it makes feel terrible about myself."*

4. Expect that anything you say when confronting a toxic person will be repeated by him or her to someone else. Moreover, it'll be done in a way designed to make you appear to be the offending party. Given this, watch what you say - and the way you say it - to him or her. As I mentioned above, don't attack the person's behavior. Just state, with honesty and respect, how it affects you.

5. Stand your ground. When you confront a toxic person to sever the relationship, anticipate a reprisal. It may come in the form of emotional manipulation (e.g. *"What kind of a person abandons a friend like this?"*). Or it might come in the form of gaslighting (e.g. *"You're crazy. I don't act in the way you've described."*). The toxic person may resort to ad hominem attacks (e.g. *"If you weren't*

so unreliable, I wouldn't be so critical.") or
diversionary measures designed to shift
attention (e.g. "*Oh, so you're saying you're perfect?*").
Be prepared to remain firm when confronted
with such tactics.

Day 12

~

Stop Being Satisfied With Mediocre Performance

MANY PEOPLE LIVE their lives as underachievers. They set low performance standards for themselves and then exert the least amount of effort possible toward meeting them. This is the case in their relationships, career, and home life. For them, a life of mediocrity is a life well lived, even though it's accompanied by an undercurrent of disappointment and discontent. Failing to reach one's potential carries a subtle, but persistent regret.

The biggest problem with settling for mediocrity is that, once that mindset gains a foothold, it infects every area of your life. Eventually, you abandon your dreams and goals. You allow your relationships to atrophy from inattention. You give up on your pursuits for personal and professional growth. Before long, the "virus" of mediocrity has taken over the entire host, polluting everything from your willpower and focus to your physical health.

No doubt you can imagine how this predicament destroys your productivity.

How This Bad Habit Hurts Your Productivity

WHEN WE'RE willing to settle for less than we're capable of doing, it's easy to become stuck in a rut. Moreover, there's a seductive comfort to remaining so. When we're in a rut, we never allow ourselves to be challenged so we never have to worry about failure. Everything we do while we're in this state is well within our comfort zone.

The downside is that we sacrifice personal and professional growth. Without venturing outside our comfort zone, we miss opportunities to expand our skillset and broaden our knowledge. This might, at first, seem acceptable because it implies we'll be an expert in the skills and knowledge we currently possess. In reality, it erodes our contributory value - to our friends, family members, and employers. If we fail to grow, we lose ground as the world changes around us. We ultimately have less comparative value to offer.

When we embrace mediocrity, we also become less aware of our weaknesses. We develop a type of tunnel vision that obfuscates how we perceive ourselves. Deficits are dismissed as irrelevant because they're unnecessary to our current processes. From this insular perspective, because there's no urgency to pursue growth, there's no need to be concerned about our deficits. Meanwhile, the gap that separates our capabilities from our potential becomes a veritable chasm as the world around us evolves.

If you're tired of living a life of mediocrity, and are

ready to strive for more, here's how to do it. Don't be surprised if your productivity soars as a result.

Action Steps

1. Envision the type of person you'd like to become. Do you want to be successful? Do you wish to be a leader? Would you like to be filled with a sense of personal achievement? Would you like others to see you as honest, reliable, compassionate, and principled? This image will be your archetype. It'll serve as an amalgamation of all the traits and accomplishments to which you aspire. If you feel like you're losing your way, recall this image to help yourself to get back on track.

2. Seek a coach or mentor. This person should exhibit some of the traits you want to develop. He or she should also have accomplished feats that are similar to those you want to accomplish. Model your choices and your behaviors after this individual. This isn't to suggest you become a carbon copy of the person. Rather, recognize the decisions that contributed to his or her results, and incorporate them into your life taking into account your personal circumstances.

3. Pledge to do your best whenever you devote

your attention to something. This step may require you to make a subtle change in your values. In the past, you may have been content to do the bare minimum, just enough to get by. But that position must change. You must now commit to excellence. Strive to do things better than you've done them in the past.

4. Be willing to take on tasks and projects that no one else is willing to absorb. Others' reticence may stem from a belief that a particular task is too hard, unpleasant, or impossible to do well. Take the opportunity to venture outside your comfort zone. Task failure is irrelevant since you're the only one stepping forward to take it on. As a bonus, you'll inspire others' respect, which, in turn, will motivate you to continue performing at a level that warrants it.

5. Reduce your TV time by 50%. Watching television is good way to unwind after a tough day. But most of us spend too much time in front of our TVs. We sit down with the intention to watch one or two episodes of our favorite show, and end up binge-watching for several hours. This can be disastrous if you're already struggling to break the habit of accepting mediocrity. Take a look at all of the shows you're currently watching. Pick the one that means the least to you and stop watching it.

Pick another the following week. And another the week after that one.

6. Adjust your schedule so you're able to go to bed a little earlier each evening and wake up a little earlier each morning. Doing so gives you an immediate sense of control over your life. The idea is that if you can control this one thing, you can control *other* things. And that means you have influence over your life. You don't have to settle for mediocrity. You can *choose* the life you want to live.

Day 13

Stop Fearing Failure

NO ONE LIKES TO FAIL. Being unable to measure up, either to our own expectations or those of others, is demoralizing. If it happens over and over, it can be downright depressing. It's no wonder so many of us will do just about anything to avoid it.

But if you peel back the layers of the human psyche, you'll see that the *fear* of failure is rooted in unhealthy anxieties. For example, we worry about what other people will think of us if we fail. We agonize over disappointing them and having them form negative opinions of us. Along the way, we become convinced of our inadequacies, not due to hard evidence, but rather the unjustifiable assertions of our inner critics.

And so, when confronted with an unfamiliar task or project (or one we've botched in the past), we become paralyzed. We freeze up, unable to act because we've undermined ourselves and our abilities, usually without justification. This fear dominates our mind space, increasing our stress and pummeling our confidence.

How This Bad Habit Hurts Your Productivity

I REFER to the fear of failure as a habit because it forms over time. Like smoking, overindulgence in video games, and lack of punctuality, it's a learned pattern. It develops as part of a routine that become entrenched with repetition.

The causes of fear of failure vary from person to person. For many of us, its origin can be traced back to our childhoods. But whatever its genesis, its *impact* on our lives is easy to recognize.

Fear of failure causes us to procrastinate. When we're faced with tasks that lie beyond our comfort zones, we stall for time. In some cases, we stall indefinitely, secretly hoping the tasks in question will magically go away.

Fear of failure prevents us from taking on projects that challenge us. We stick closely to what we know, thereby eliminating risk, but sacrifice opportunities for personal and professional growth.

Fear of failure encourages perfectionism. We refuse to take on tasks and projects unless we know we can perform them perfectly. Oftentimes, this means refusing to take them on altogether.

Fear of failure adversely impacts our ability to make quick decisions. We become so concerned about making a *wrong* decision that we end up making no decision at all.

The purpose of fear is to protect us from harm. But fear of failure sabotages us, preventing us from enjoying meaningful success. Following is an action plan for overcoming this habit and embracing risk as a necessary component in achieving personal growth.

Action Steps

1. Recognize the fear. It's not always obvious because it resides deep in our psyches. It only appears to do its dirty work, and then it fades away to lie in wait until we're once again confronted with a challenging task. Acknowledge that the fear exists.
2. Come to terms with the fact that failure is an ever-present risk in anything you do. It's even possible to fail when handling things at which you're adept.
3. Think of failures as mere setbacks. They're not final judgements on your potential. On the contrary, they're stepping stones to success. Setbacks are terrific learning opportunities if you allow yourself to see them as such. They highlight what works and what doesn't work, giving you actionable insight you can use in future endeavors.
4. Be willing to fail fast. If setbacks are learning opportunities, doesn't it seem sensible to accelerate the process? The faster you learn what works and what doesn't work, the faster you can adjust and make forward progress.

5. Create a reward program. Select several rewards that range from small to large. Whenever you do something that requires you to step outside your comfort zone, reward yourself in a manner that's commensurate with your discomfort. For example, if you tackle a small task you've been dreading, allow yourself to spend 10 minutes on Facebook. The risk is small and so is the reward. If you take on a big project that seems overwhelming to you, reward yourself with tickets to see your favorite band or orchestra in concert. Bigger risk, bigger reward. The idea is to train your brain to associate the acceptance of risk with an immediate reward. This association will gradually overpower, and ultimately quash, your fear of failure. It takes time, but be patient with yourself. It *will* happen.

6. Stop blaming yourself. It's one thing to take responsibility for your actions and decisions. Doing so is essential to growth. It's another thing entirely to immediately blame and mercilessly berate yourself for your mistakes. Without question, you should investigate the causes of your setbacks. That's how you gain actionable insight, essential to making purposeful adjustments in how you approach things down the road. But casting blame for its own sake is purposeless. Worse, it's likely to

aggravate your fear of failure. Stop playing the blame game.

7. Consider the worst-case scenario. Our fear and dread often cause us to imagine unrealistic outcomes. Under scrutiny, it quickly becomes clear that these outcomes are highly unlikely to occur. For example, as a shy teenager, I was deathly afraid to approach girls. In the dark recesses of my fearful mind, I imagined being ridiculed in front of my classmates and driven away in shame. But that expectation was unrealistic. In truth, the worst that would plausibly happen is that a girl would be standoffish. And I found that I could handle *that* response with poise and grace. Once you confront the *true* worst-case scenario of taking action, you'll find that taking action is far less daunting.

Day 14

~

Stop Fearing Success

FEAR OF SUCCESS can cause just as much anxiety as fear of failure. It springs from a few sources. Some people fear success because they're uncertain how to cope with the aftereffects. An example is a musician who worries about the demands of stardom should his music skyrocket to the top of the bestseller charts.

Others fear success because they're concerned that it'll change them in some distinctive way. An example is an executive who worries that a string of promotions and raises will erode his humility.

Still others fear success because they assume it demonstrates they've sacrificed their principles in some manner to achieve it. An example is an attorney who worries that taking certain types of cases, while lucrative, will compromise his or her ethics.

Whatever its origin, a fear of success will hold you back from reaching your potential. It'll discourage you from pursuing your goals, taking on bigger responsibilities, and making a notable impact on those around you.

How This Bad Habit Hurts Your Productivity

FEAR OF SUCCESS causes us to procrastinate. When faced with a project for which success might result in recognition, praise, and greater authority and culpability, we delay taking action. As long as we refuse to move forward, there's no risk of success. And that means we can ignore the after-effects of success that concern us.

Fear of success can also discourage us from doing our best work. If we're worried that our best work will result in greater responsibilities and loftier expectations, we may be inclined to put in less effort.

This fear can cause us to behave in other self-sabotaging ways. At our jobs, we may start showing up late, stop contributing in meetings, and become acerbic to our coworkers. At home, we might ignore our household duties, squander our money, and lose our temper with our loved ones.

The worst part is, fear of success is easy to overlook because it often develops and ferments at a subconscious level. So our self-sabotaging behaviors might be automatic responses, and thus happening without our understanding the reasons.

If you harbor a fear of success, it's almost certainly hampering your productivity and holding you back. Here's how to overcome it…

Action Steps

1. Realize the fear isn't about success. It's about the perceived *side effects* of success. Some of these side effects may indeed be undesirable to you. The question is, how likely are they to occur and do you have any control over them? For example, suppose you're worried that hosting a successful party will cause your friends to think of you as the default host for every subsequent get-together. It's an obligation you'd like to avoid. First, ask yourself whether your friends would *really* react in that way. Second, in the unlikely event they do so, remind yourself that you can refuse to become the default host.

2. Identify the side effects of success that concern you. Oftentimes, fear of success is shrouded in - and empowered by - uncertainty. We're uncertain about what worries us, and so the fear remains vague. In order to confront and overcome our worries, we must first know what they are. For example, suppose you'd like to write a novel. Do you fear success because you're concerned you'll attract negative reviews? Are you worried that you'll draw trolls who revel in disparaging others' work? Once you've identified the side effects that concern you, you can rationally address them one by one.

3. Recall past successes and think about their repercussions. For example, you may have

cooked an amazing meal for your family. Were there any negative effects? Or you might have received a perfect score on a mid-term exam. Did anything bad happen as a result of that accomplishment? Or perhaps you delivered a perfect presentation at your job. Did that success lead to regrettable consequences? The answer will almost always be "no." The purpose of this step is to whittle away the unreasonable expectation that success will end badly for you.

4. Write down how the fear of success is holding you back. Is it limiting your career opportunities? Is it preventing you from finding the man or woman of your dreams? Is it discouraging you from making the most of your time, money, and other resources? This exercise is important because your circumstances are unique. Consequently, the ways in which fear of success prevents you achieving your potential are unique. Writing down the specifics gives them form, which makes them easier to address.

5. Write in a personal journal. Our fears, along with the feelings that accompany them, reside in our minds. That's where they enjoy their greatest influence and wield their greatest power over us. Journaling gives you an opportunity to transfer those fears and feelings

to paper (or an online platform like Evernote or OneNote). When you document them, you can more easily focus on details you'd otherwise miss. Remember, most fears and feelings wield power because of their ambiguity. Journaling allows you to define and ruminate about the specifics.

6. Develop the habit of positive self-talk. Remind yourself each day of your strengths, abilities, and willingness to work hard. Note that you deserve success based on these merits. For example, if you're a terrific host, you *deserve* to host a terrific party. If you're a talented songwriter, you *deserve* to see others enjoy your music. If you're an amazing parent, you *deserve* to watch your child grow up to be happy, confident, and resilient. Too often, our fear of success discourages us from believing that we're *worthy* of success. Use positive self-talk to remind yourself that you've earned it.

∽

Stop Neglecting To Prioritize Tasks, Projects, And Relationships

WHEN YOU START WORKING each day, whether at home or your workplace, do you start by tackling your highest-priority task? When deciding whether to spend time with someone, do you consider the importance you place on that relationship? If you neglect to prioritize these things, you'll end up spending your limited time and energy on negligible pursuits. This time and energy, once spent, will no longer be available for pursuits that are truly consequential to you.

Prioritization allows us to manage our resources. Since we have limited time available, it's important that we spend it on the activities and relationships that carry the greatest impact. Since we possess a limited amount of attentional energy, it's crucial that we devote it to important tasks that require concentration.

Neglecting to prioritize our tasks, projects, and relationships causes us to squander our resources. When we mismanage these resources, we become less effective and less efficient.

How This Bad Habit Hurts Your Productivity

WHEN YOU FAIL TO PRIORITIZE, everything in your life takes on the same level of urgency. Trivial tasks seem no less important than crucial ones. Extraneous relationships seem as significant as those that are unquestionably vital to your happiness and wellbeing. This leads to stress as you begin to feel overwhelmed, trying to meet competing demands for your attention. As we noted in *Day 10*, persistent stress reduces productivity.

Lack of prioritization also causes you to waste valuable time. Without identifying which tasks, projects, and relationships most deserve your attention, you'll inevitably end up spending time on the nonessential. This can have disastrous results when you're working under aggressive deadlines.

When everything in your life has the same level of urgency, it's tempting to start jumping from one task to the next before you complete anything. This ruins your workflow, which, in turn, hampers your productivity.

Lastly, lack of prioritization creates a time management emergency. At our jobs, tasks and projects accumulate as deadlines loom. At home, relational demands pile up, often when the most important people in your life need your attention. Left with insufficient time and energy to address all of the demands, you cut corners out of necessity. Consequently, the quality of your work suffers, and the connections you share with your friends and loved ones erode.

Prioritizing the demands on your time and energy brings order to chaos. It also gives you a way to filter out the unimportant demands so you'll possess the necessary resources to address the ones that truly matter to you. Here's how to get started.

Action Steps

1. Acknowledge that you have time and attentional constraints. Few of us have enough time and energy to address every demand placed upon us. But it's not until we admit as much that we can truly prioritize our lives. If we don't openly acknowledge our constraints, it's easy to fall into the trap of thinking we can do everything and please everyone.

2. Think about your values and goals. These will determine what you consider to be important. Ask yourself: what do you want to achieve in your life, and why do you want to achieve these things? Who do you most value in your life, and why do you value them so highly? Recognize that not every task, project, and relationship is equally important. This becomes clear when you think about them in the context of your principles and aspirations.

3. Realize that if you fail to prioritize your life, someone else will inevitably do it for you. Many people spend their valuable time responding to others' needs rather than addressing their own. They react to the world around them rather than living with purpose and intention. Be willing to say no to the demands others try to place on you. Doing so will free up your time and other resources to devote to what is actually important to you.

4. Create to-do lists and prioritize each item. If you're already doing so, you're ahead of the game. Otherwise, start today. Write down every task and relational obligation that needs your attention. Then, go down the list and assign one of three priorities for each item based on its importance and urgency. Keep it simple by using an A-B-C or 1-2-3 protocol. Critical items should receive an "A" or "1." Important, non-urgent items should receive a "B" or "2." Trivial items should receive a "C" or "3." This practice allows you to scan your to-do list and quickly identify which items to focus on.

5. Consider the consequences of inaction. What is the worst that can happen if you fail to act on a particular to-do list item? Will you be unable to complete other items or address other relational demands? Will your inaction prevent you from achieving your goals? This exercise will help to

clarify where you should spend your time and
energy.

6. Avoid allowing others' priorities to become your
own. At the office, coworkers may try to
wrangle your help to complete *their* projects,
even if it forces you to temporarily abandon
yours. At home, family members will try to enlist
your help toward achieving *their* ends, even if
those ends fail to align with your own. Your
friends might demand your time due to matters
that are urgent to *them*, even if that means you
have to drop whatever you're working on. Some
situations warrant adjusting your priorities in
favor of someone else's priorities. But such
situations are rare.

7. Understand the difference between urgent and
important. Just because a task or relational
demand is urgent doesn't mean it warrants your
immediate attention. First, urgency often stems
from eagerness or enthusiasm rather than a true
need for swift action. For example, you might
receive an "urgent" text from a friend asking
you to call her immediately. Upon calling her,
you learn that she wants to tell you about her
latest family drama. While this drama may be
urgent (to your friend, at least), it's arguably
unimportant to you. Second, urgency is often
expressed in others' needs. For example, a

coworker may approach you, panicked about a looming deadline he's unable to meet. He implores you to help him. While his situation may indeed be urgent (and perhaps important) to *him*, neither may be the case for *you*.

Day 16

~

Stop Taking Too Long To Make Decisions

MAKING DECISIONS PRECEDES TAKING ACTION. The former must happen before the latter becomes possible. That being the case, indecision *impedes* taking action. It thwarts your ability to get things done.

Indecision can occur for a number of reasons. Having too many options is a common cause. The more options we have, the more difficult it is to choose from among them.

Laziness is another common reason. We feel sluggish and idle, and avoid making decisions as a way to avoid having to exert effort.

Many perfectionists struggle with indecisiveness. If they delay making a decision, they can delay taking action on challenging tasks that present the risk of failure (or even imperfection).

Others are indecisive because they fear taking ownership of their decisions and bearing responsibility for the consequences. If they delay making a decision, they can avoid taking the blame for anything that goes wrong as a result of that decision.

Still others avoid making decisions because they lack a clear purpose, one driven by their goals and values. They're uncertain regarding what they want to achieve, and so they stall because they're apprehensive regarding where their decisions will lead.

As you can imagine, constant indecision makes it nearly impossible to be effective and productive over prolonged periods.

How This Bad Habit Hurts Your Productivity

INDECISION CAN HARM your productivity more than most bad habits. First, it whittles away your confidence. Each time you're unable to make a decision, your inner critic gains leverage it then uses to attack your competence. The more it happens, the worse you feel about yourself.

Second, overthinking things causes you to miss opportunities. For example, suppose you're given a chance to work on a high-profile project at your job. But instead of agreeing to join the project team, you hem and haw until the opportunity is no longer available. You've missed it, along with its attendant benefits (e.g. exposure to important people within your organization, a chance to broaden your skills and knowledge, etc.).

Third, indecisiveness allows time to slip through your fingers. Parkinson's law states that "work expands so as to fill the time available for its completion." If you're unable to make decisions, you'll be left idle while time continues to tick away. Consequently, everything you do will take longer than should be the case.

Fourth, it impairs your working memory. Your working memory is like a computer's RAM (random access memory). It's where your mind temporarily stores information for later processing. Like a computer's RAM, working memory is in limited supply. The problem is, as we noted above, the more options you have in front of you, the harder it is to choose. And that indecision causes you to experience pressure and stress. Pressure and stress tax your working memory[1], leaving fewer resources available to process information.

If you struggle with indecision, you know firsthand how it affects your productivity. Following is a simple strategy for learning to make smarter decisions *faster*.

Action Steps

1. Accept that a sacrifice is always necessary. We're often averse to making a decision because we fear missing out on something we want. For example, suppose there are two films currently in theaters that you want to see. You only have time to see one of them. This predicament can cause you to freeze with indecision. Once you accept that you cannot have everything you want, it'll become easier to move forward with a purposeful decision.

2. Recognize that researching something ad nauseam doesn't mean you'll make a better decision. Additional information can *confuse* as easily as it can elucidate or clarify. When you're faced with making a decision with incomplete information, trust your instincts. Admittedly, this is easier said than done, especially if you're unaccustomed to doing so. But like all habits, it becomes easier the more you do it.

3. Give yourself a time limit. It's okay to be indecisive. The world's top business icons, military leaders, and experts in every imaginable field sometimes find it difficult to choose from among competing options. But at some point, a decision must be made. Force the issue by putting a deadline on the item that depends on your decision. For example, suppose you'd like to put your home up for sale, but are uncertain regarding which real estate agent you'd like to hire. Set a non-negotiable deadline by which to list your home. The deadline will spur you to choose an agent.

4. Acknowledge that some decisions will turn out badly. This can occur even when you have all of the relevant information at your disposal. When you accept the fact that some outcomes are beyond your control, making decisions becomes less daunting. For example, suppose you're trying to choose a restaurant to visit this

weekend with your spouse. Admit that even the most informed choice can have terrible results (e.g. inattentive service, food poisoning, etc.). Doing so relieves the pressure and stress with which you'd otherwise burden yourself.

5. Tackle your most difficult decisions early in the day. Decisions sap our willpower. As the day progresses, and we make more and more decisions, our willpower evaporates until little remains. This is the reason simple decisions - e.g. what to have for dinner, whether to go to the gym, and which movie to rent - are challenging at the end of the day. It's not just you. Everyone experiences this. Tackling hard decisions early in the day will help you to avoid "paralysis by analysis." You'll make smarter decisions faster and be able to move forward with confidence.

6. Develop a habit for making fast decisions. Start with decisions that carry small consequences, such as where you'll eat lunch or what to wear to the office. Small stakes will make it easier to take action without overthinking things. The purpose of this exercise is to train yourself to make snap decisions. The decisions may not be completely informed, and the results may be less than ideal, but that's okay. The important thing is that you'll develop a habit that'll short circuit your tendency to vacillate.

[1]
https://www.ncbi.nlm.nih.gov/pmc/articles/PMC262859
2/

Day 17

◠

Stop Quitting Bad Habits Cold Turkey

QUITTING habits cold turkey is associated with a success-or-failure mindset. This mindset champions the idea that we either have what it takes to succeed or we don't. There's no middle ground.

This attitude sets you up for failure. It encourages perfectionism and gives rise to unreasonable expectations. It pushes you to adopt an extremist outlook, where a single stumble on the road to overcoming a bad habit equals failure.

Cold turkey *can* work. But even when it does so, success is often fleeting. You may know this from experience. Have you ever successfully quit a bad habit cold turkey only to see it return with a vengeance days or weeks later? Many people - for example, dieters - go through this cycle over and over. Falling off the wagon becomes a bad habit in and of itself.

Personally, I fail nearly every time I attempt to quit a bad habit cold turkey. So I've stopped doing so. Instead, I've found that I enjoy greater success quitting bad habits when I take the time to cut back on them bit by bit. I'll show you how to do this in a moment. First, let's explore how quitting habits cold turkey affects your productivity.

How This Bad Habit Hurts Your Productivity

THE EFFECTS of this habit on your productivity are subtle, and thus difficult to pinpoint if you're not looking for them. First, because quitting cold turkey so often ends in failure, the bad habits that hold you back linger. If these habits affect your ability to properly manage your time, they'll be a continuous drag on your efficiency.

Even when you manage to overcome a bad habit cold turkey, there's a high likelihood of a relapse. The willpower you used in beating the habit has a limited shelf life. Once it's depleted, the habit is likely to return. This is because *true* habit change, which involves modifying the *pattern* (cue, routine, and reward) that supports the underlying habit, hasn't occurred. In most cases, it's overshadowed by the application of willpower.

Second, each time your cold-turkey adventure ends in failure, it sends a message to your brain. This message highlights your inability to deliver lasting, positive results. It's music to your inner critic's ears. Your inner critic will use the message as support for its claims that you're incompetent and ineffectual. Your self-confidence will come under repeated attack, and you'll become slowly convinced that your inner critic is correct. For example, consider a friend or family member who has tried to lose weight over and over, but failed to do so. You may have heard this individual complain, "I just can't lose weight." His or her inner critic has essentially won the battle.

Third, trying to quit bad habits cold turkey encourages you to avoid making mistakes at all costs. Remember, this process promotes an all-or-nothing mindset. You either *do* the bad habit or you *break* the habit. You either succeed or you fall off the wagon, signaling total failure. There's zero latitude for anything in between.

This is a form of perfectionism. When you adopt an all-or-nothing perspective, you become highly resistant to making mistakes. Consequently, you become averse to tackling new challenges as doing so requires leaving your comfort zone and risking failure. This prevents you from experiencing personal and professional growth.

I recommend an easier, more forgiving, and in my opinion, more effective approach to quitting bad habits. It always works for me, and I'm confident it'll work for you, too.

Action Steps

1. Identify the bad habit. This may sound like banal advice, but it's easy to overlook the habit and focus on the undesirable result. For example, an individual trying to lose weight might overlook his penchant for bread, and instead focus on the numbers he sees on his

scale. An executive trying to get more things done might overlook his habit of responding immediately to texts and emails, and instead focus on his unfinished to-do list. Identify the habit you'd like to break. This is a simple, but crucial step.

2. Pinpoint the cues that trigger the habit. For example, do you visit Facebook every time you're bored? If so, boredom is the trigger. Do you reach for junk food whenever you're feeling stressed? If so, stress is the trigger. Are you tempted to watch television at a certain time each day? In this case, the time of day is the trigger. These cues are part of a neurological loop. They prompt behavior, usually at a subconscious level. Once you've identified the cues, you can create a plan to interrupt the loop. An interruption can come in the form of cue avoidance (e.g. taking steps to reduce stress) or response modification (e.g. chatting with a coworker rather than eating junk food when you're stressed).

3. Design a 4-week action plan. Ideally, we'd be able to break bad habits in a single day through sheer willpower, confident they'll never return. Unfortunately, that's not how habit change works. Our minds need time to adopt new routines. In many cases, the neurological loops that support our bad habits have existed for

years. It'll take time to modify them. Create a plan that details the actions you'll take each day to break the habit in question. It can be as simple as *"visit Sharon's cubicle when I feel stressed."*

4. Take small steps. Your 4-week action plan will go a long way toward implementing this tactic. During the four weeks, you'll gradually wean yourself from the bad habit. For example, suppose you typically visit Facebook whenever you're bored. Each session lasts for 20 minutes. During the first few days, cut the duration of these sessions in half, to 10 minutes. During the next few days, cut it in half again, to five minutes. During the following week, alternate between spending five minutes on Facebook with another activity. An example might be to call a friend for a chat. Or you might focus your attention on completing tiny tasks, such as making a dentist appointment or dinner reservation. The purpose is to modify your response to the existing cue. Your brain will slowly acclimate to the modified pattern, helping you to ultimately break your Facebook habit that's triggered by boredom.

5. Keep a habit journal. In the morning, write down your intentions for the day regarding the habit in question. In the evening, write down whether you managed to avoid the habit

throughout that day. Your journal entries need not be long. A few sentences will suffice.

6. Forgive yourself when you stumble. True habit change almost always involves mistakes. For example, suppose that despite your intention to avoid junk food, you eat a pastry tomorrow upon feeling stressed. Don't reprimand yourself. Recognize that you made a mistake, forgive yourself, and renew your commitment to your goal (e.g. breaking your junk food habit). Many accomplishments are achieved only after a series of blunders. Don't shortchange yourself by accepting failure after a single slip. Successful habit change is about repetition and routine, not perfection.

~

Stop Trying To Make Too Many Changes At Once

MOST OF US would like to change multiple things in our lives. For example, we'd like to eat better, get more exercise, improve our focus, quit coffee, give up refined carbs, develop more confidence, overcome procrastination, save more money, wake up earlier, and read more non-fiction. That's just scratching the surface, but you get the idea.

It's tempting to jump in headfirst and tackle all of our habit-based aspirations at once. Doing so seems like the quickest path toward achieving transformative change in our lives. But in reality, the opposite is true. Making too many changes at once practically ensures that good habits will fail to stick and bad habits will continue to linger.

Why? Because it's easy to become overwhelmed with the attendant requirements of the changes you're trying to make. And when you feel overwhelmed, you're more inclined to give up. With that in mind, let's talk about how this approach to habit change makes you less productive.

How This Bad Habit Hurts Your Productivity

WHENEVER YOU ATTEMPT to change an existing behavioral pattern, you can expect to face internal resistance. Your mind is accustomed to your current routines. It enjoys the status quo and resists changes, even if the changes are beneficial in the long run. This is one of the reasons true habit change can be such a major challenge. The mind is a formidable opponent.

Now, imagine trying to change a dozen behavioral patterns at the same time. Your mind will revolt, throwing up roadblocks at every turn. Where a single habit change was a challenge, a dozen changes become impractical. The effort is doomed from the start, and the time and energy spent, both of which could have been used more productively, is wasted.

Another problem is that it's difficult to evaluate results when you're trying to make multiple changes at once. This is especially true when the changes share an association. For example, suppose you'd like to quit coffee, give up processed sugar, and incorporate routines designed to reduce stress. These three things affect your temperament. Quitting coffee can trigger withdrawal symptoms that cause irritability. Giving up sugar can trigger anxiety and fatigue. Both can increase your stress levels even as you employ measures to *reduce* your stress.

In this scenario, it'd be difficult to know whether you're making headway. For example, suppose you're experiencing stress. Does this mean you've failed to properly implement effective stress-reducing routines, or is the stress related to giving up coffee and sugar? It's impossible to pinpoint causation with certainty. That means there's no way to tell whether your efforts and energy have been sensibly deployed.

Yet another problem is that trying to change too many things at once slows down new pattern adoption and acclimation. Because you'll confront internal resistance with every attempt to change existing patterns, you'll be devoting significant mental energy to the effort. These attentional resources become spread too thinly. Consequently, it takes longer to establish new patterns and have them take root. Indeed, the new patterns may fail to take root at all if there aren't sufficient cognitive resources to attend to the process.

You probably know someone who tried to change multiple habits in his or her life at once. It's almost certain those habits failed to stick. Transformative change *is* possible. But it requires a different approach than the one examined above. Following are the core highlights.

Action Steps

1. Write down every habit you'd like to change. Small, large, and everything in between. Include good habits you'd like to adopt as well as bad habits you'd like to overcome. You may be tempted to keep this list in your head. Don't. Write it down so you can review it, take notes, and make changes as they become

necessary or appropriate given your circumstances.

2. Assign a difficulty level, from one to five, for each habit. One means extreme difficulty and five means minimal difficulty. For example, you might assign a "1" to "quit smoking" and a "5" to "read more non-fiction."

3. Commit to changing a single habit at a time. You may think you can handle more. You may indeed be able to do so. But for now, commit to making one change at a time.

4. Allocate a timeframe for each habit change according to the habit's difficulty level. For example, a difficulty level of "1" may suggest that you'll need six weeks to complete the change. A difficulty level of "5" might suggest you'll only need two weeks. The timeframes you apply to each habit change will depend primarily on your cognitive resources and predilections regarding the habits in question. Quick tip: don't underestimate the amount of time you'll need to adopt new habits. Plan conservatively. It's better to allocate more time than necessary than sabotage yourself by allocating insufficient time.

5. Create an action plan for each habit change. In *Day 17* we talked about designing a 4-week action plan composed of small steps that'll guide us toward a predefined goal. Use the

same approach here. For example, suppose you'd like to read more non-fiction. You've assigned this habit change a difficulty level of "5" and determined it'll take you two weeks to adopt the new practice. Your action plan might appear as follows: Days 1 through 3 - read 10 minutes before going to bed. Days 4 through 6 - read 15 minutes before going to bed. Days 7 through 9 - read 20 minutes before going to bed. Days 10 through 14 - read 30 minutes before going to bed. Again, small steps are the key to making habit changes stick.

6. Find a support partner. This individual will hold you accountable and provide needed encouragement and inspiration. Ideally, this person will have successfully made the change you're trying to make. But that's not necessary. The important thing is that you find someone - a friend, spouse, or coach - to be in your corner. Habit change is tough enough without having to do it in isolation.

Day 19

~

Stop Letting A Lack Of Motivation Prevent You From Taking Action

WHEN I TALK about adopting good habits and eliminating bad ones, I usually highlight the importance of behavioral routines. Routines are vital to habit change because they help our brains acclimate to a new normal. They whittle down the internal resistance we face whenever we attempt to make positive changes in our lives.

Having said that, motivation can also be an important tool. It can help us to break through our lethargy and take purposeful action. It can spur us to take the first step toward positive habit change, triggering a transformative process that yields the results we desire.

The problem is, motivation is unreliable. It's influenced by a myriad f internal and external factors, many of which are beyond our control. Our relationships, financial status, energy levels, reputation among our peers, and opportunities for personal growth, along with other factors, all play a role. When some of these elements are not in our favor, our motivation plummets. This, in turn, can cause us to become idle, crippling our ability to get things done.

How This Bad Habit Hurts Your Productivity

WHEN YOU'RE UNMOTIVATED, it's difficult to work. You become trapped in a torpor, where even simple tasks cause you to feel mild dread. For example, have you ever planned to do household chores only to put them on the back burner in favor of taking a nap? Have you ever intended to complete an aggressive to-do list only to give up early and spend the time on Facebook? Or have you ever planned to visit the gym after getting home from the office only to abandon the idea in favor of watching shows on Netflix?

If so, you know firsthand that demotivation is an obstacle to taking goal-oriented action.

Lack of motivation can also stunt your personal and professional growth. It's accompanied by a lack of enthusiasm. This state erodes your eagerness to improve yourself, leaving you without the will to pursue positive changes in your life.

It also leads to an unspecific sense of dissatisfaction. When you're unmotivated and consequently lethargic, it's easy to fall into a general malaise. You'll begin to feel discontented and disappointed, but unable to identify the reasons. If this despondency persists, it'll slowly whittle away your self-confidence until you feel *unable* to take action.

Although motivation is difficult to control, it *is* possible to climb out of a demotivated slump. Following are several tips you can use to recharge your motivation when it's time to take action.

Action Steps

1. Take the first step. While we often think of motivation as the precursor to taking action, it's more often the other way around. Taking action, even just a single purposeful step, gives us the motivation we need to continue. Here's a personal example: there are times when I'm unmotivated to write. But I know from experience that once I sit down and write a few words, I'll gain the motivation to continue writing. It happens every time.

2. Create simple routines that'll prompt you to tackle specific tasks. These routines will serve as mini cues. They'll get you into the right frame of mind to take the type of action you need to take. For example, my writing routine is to read a few paragraphs written by non-fiction authors whose books I've enjoyed. If you're planning to clean your home, your routine might comprise turning the television off, drinking a glass of water, and gathering the necessary cleaning supplies. If you intend to visit the gym after work, your routine might be to don your gym clothes and do a few stretches before leaving the

house. The purpose of these routines is to train your brain to anticipate what comes next. The routines are patterns that prompt specific behaviors. The key to making them work is to do them every time you're about to tackle the tasks for which they've been created.

3. Abandon the idea of doing a perfect job. The pressure that accompanies perfectionism is a motivation killer. Give yourself permission to do an imperfect job. If you intend to clean your house, don't worry about cleaning every nook and cranny. If you're creating a presentation for your job, don't worry about being flawless. Once you deliberately reject the expectations associated with perfection, you'll have more latitude to act without concern of failure.

4. Keep track of your accomplishments, even the small ones. Oftentimes, we feel demotivated because we think we're failing to make progress toward our goals. This feeling overlooks past achievements. So maintain an "accomplishment" journal that highlights them. It doesn't matter whether you keep this journal online (using an app like Evernote or OneNote) or on a pad of paper. The important thing is that you're able to refer to it whenever you feel unmotivated. A quick reminder of your past achievements may be all you need to garner the resolve to take action.

5. Organize your workspace. Clutter can sap our motivation to take purposeful action. It's difficult to focus and work productively when we see chaos reigning in our office or on our desk. The disorganization can be daunting. If this describes your workspace, spend five minutes clearing away the clutter. Get rid of papers you no longer need. Put odds and ends into a small box and set it aside, preferably out of sight. Decide later whether to keep or discard the items. You may find that the clutter and disorder was siphoning your will to act. Clearing it away and reintroducing tidiness can help you to break free of your lethargy.

Day 20

~

Stop Refusing To Commit To Your Goals

IN THE CONTEXT of achieving goals, commitment can be defined as devotion to a particular outcome. For example, you might be committed to decluttering your home. Or perhaps you're committed to learning a new language. Or maybe you're committed to securing five new clients this month at your job. The point is that you have an outcome in mind and are *dedicated* to making it happen.

The problem is, it's easy to confuse commitment with mere interest. When this occurs, our aspirations wither on the vine. For example, it's been nearly thirty years since I've played the guitar, and I've aspired to start playing again. But I'm not *committed* to this goal. I'm merely interested in it. That being the case, you won't be surprised to hear that it hasn't happened.

In contrast, I decided late last year that I wanted to publish four books within twelve months. I made a personal commitment to this goal. I vowed to make it happen. Consequently, the book you're currently reading is the fourth book I've published in the last twelve months.

Each day, we're faced with a palette of goals. Some are small, manifesting as daily to-do items. Others are large, reflecting our long-term aspirations. If we refuse to commit to them, we can hardly expect to achieve them. The more likely result is that we won't enjoy the outcomes we desire.

How This Bad Habit Hurts Your Productivity

WHEN WE REFUSE to commit to a particular outcome, we're less likely to bring that outcome to pass. Above, I gave the example of my interest in playing the guitar. I've harbored this interest for more than three years. Yet in that time, I've done nothing to advance that goal. I refused to commit to it, and thus I've made no forward progress.

Often, our refusal to commit causes us to take more time than necessary to complete important tasks and projects. For example, suppose you intend to clean your home. It's not a project you can simply abandon. At some point, you'll need to address the accumulated clutter, dust, grime, and debris. If you fail to commit to the undertaking, you'll be inclined to put it off. When you finally tackle it, you'll do so without enthusiasm. And that'll only result in your working more slowly.

Lack of commitment can also cause us to miss deadlines. Consider how efficiently you work when you possess determination and singleminded focus. Your productivity soars. Moreover, you're able to easily meet deadlines, even aggressive ones. The opposite happens when you refuse to commit. You approach tasks and projects in a halfhearted manner. You may also struggle with distractions because you haven't dedicated your attentional resources to the task at hand.

Failing to finish projects, taking longer than necessary to complete tasks, and missing deadlines... all of these indicate diminished productivity. With this in mind, let's explore how to commit ourselves to our goals and take intentional, enthusiastic action toward achieving them.

Action Steps

1. Figure out what you'd like to accomplish. Specificity is key. For example, it's not enough for me to want to "play the guitar." Instead, I should specify that I want to play faster, smoother, and with more flavor and better improvisational skills. Likewise, it's not enough to want to "clean your home." Instead, specify that you want to declutter the living room, clean the kitchen countertops, and sweep the porch.

2. Determine *why* you want to accomplish the goal in question. For example, I might want to expertly play the guitar because creating music relieves my stress and makes me happy. You may wish to clean your home because you're

expecting dinner guests later in the week. An executive might want to declutter his office because doing so will allow him to focus and complete important work faster. Isolating the reasons that compel us to act gives us clarity regarding whether our actions align with our values and desires.

3. Create a list of activities and aspirations you'll need to abandon if you decide to commit to the goal in question. For example, recall my goal of writing four books within twelve months. I recognized in advance that this goal would be possible only if I made certain sacrifices. To that end, I watched fewer shows on Netflix, I saw my family and friends less frequently, and I relegated playing the guitar to the back burner. I could only truly commit to my goal after I had identified the things I would need to forego. Go through the same process when deciding whether to truly commit to a particular outcome.

4. Brainstorm potential stumbling blocks. If we identify them ahead of time, we'll be less likely to give up in the event we encounter them. Instead, we'll be inclined to persevere because we prepared ourselves. For example, suppose you need to create a presentation for your job. One potential hurdle might be learning the software program that'll display your charts,

graphs, and other visuals. Another may be a lack of access to crucial data needed for your presentation. Yet another might be scheduling your presentation so that key people within your organization can attend. It's easy to crumble when faced with unanticipated problems. Considering such problems in advance prepares you. It also encourages the flexibility you'll need to come up with creative solutions and ultimately achieve your desired outcome.

5. Think about the resources you'll need, not just to achieve your desired outcome, but also to resolve issues along the way. Let's return to our example of creating a presentation for your job. You'll need data, content, software for creating visuals, audiovisual equipment, and help to get the word out regarding the time and place (and login details, if appropriate). You may need to tap into another person's skills and expertise for parts of your presentation. If this is your first presentation, you may need assistance setting everything up so it progresses smoothly.

6. Decide whether you are ready and willing to make a commitment. If you've completed Action Steps 1 through 5, you now recognize everything that'll be involved in achieving a particular outcome. You'll also be aware of every challenge you'll face along the way. You can now make an informed decision. Ask

yourself how committed you are to this goal in light of the expected demands on your time, energy, and attention, as well as the potential hurdles. If you decide to commit with this outlook, you'll be ready to design a reasonable action plan.

~

Stop Seeking Instant Gratification

WHEN WE DESIRE SOMETHING, we want it *now*. We'll wait if we have no other option. But if the choice is to experience gratification in the present versus experiencing it in the future, we'll typically choose the former.

For example, suppose you can either watch your favorite television program immediately or watch it later, and your decision will have no impact on your life whatsoever. Wouldn't you choose to watch it now?

Or suppose it's Tuesday and you can either go out for drinks with friends or get a good night's rest. If you knew your choice would have zero effect on your ability to function the following day, wouldn't you be tempted to go out with your friends?

In the absence of future consequences, our self-interest compels us to pursue instant gratification. Of course, in reality, there are always consequences. Life is comprised of an endless series of choices where our decisions carry repercussions. For example, if we choose to watch our favorite television show in the present, we may have to forego exercising, studying, or completing our to-do lists. If we go out drinking with our friends on a work night, we may be unable to focus and work productively the following day.

The problem is, many people find the lure of instant gratification to be irresistible. They pursue it *despite* the consequences. The idea of delaying their gratification is anathema to them, and they're willing to accept the consequences as the price for their self-indulgence.

How This Bad Habit Hurts Your Productivity

INDULGENCE in immediate gratification is often a form of self-sabotage. First, it consumes valuable time, causing it to be unavailable for more productive pursuits. If you choose to play video games, the time you spend doing so cannot be used to study for an exam. If you decide to watch television, that time will no longer be available for addressing household chores. Time is a finite resource; once it's used, it's gone forever.

Second, pursuing instant gratification encourages impulsiveness. It trains the brain to forego long-term benefits for short-term pleasure. Over time, this behavior becomes a habit, eroding our self-discipline and resilience. We become less inclined to stick to our goals and aspirations, instead surrendering to our impulses when we encounter challenges.

Third, constantly responding to the siren call of immediate gratification ultimately leads to dissatisfaction. While we feel content in the present, this feeling comes as a high price: unhappiness down the road. We begin to take things for granted, become less tolerant of unfavorable circumstances, and adopt unproductive behaviors. We also become more prone to distractions, which erode our focus, impairing our ability to complete important work.

If you struggle with the constant lure of instant gratification, it's time to start exerting control over your impulses. You'll find that delaying your short-term urges will boost your productivity, help you to make better decisions, and increase your resilience to obstacles as you pursue your goals.

Action Steps

1. Write down your biggest temptations. Focus on those that threaten to sabotage your goals. For example, you might have difficulty ignoring your phone when you receive texts and emails, even though you know they're distractions that can harm your productivity. Maybe you find junk food irresistible, even though you know eating it can derail your diet. Perhaps you check Facebook and Instagram dozens of times each day, knowing that doing so prevents you from gaining the momentum you need to get through your to-do list. Before we can control our urges, we must be acutely aware of them.

2. Create a list of your short-term, medium-term, and long-term goals and priorities. Having this list in front of you will remind you of the things you consider to be important. It'll clarify what you're choosing to sacrifice by pursuing immediate gratification. The decision to surrender to our impulses is often done in a haze of uncertainty. It's easy to overlook or underestimate the price. This list shines a spotlight on every decision, making you aware of the attendant consequences.

3. Practice delaying gratification when you face your biggest temptations. Start with small delays, and gradually increase them with time. For example, suppose you habitually check and respond to texts and emails the moment they arrive. For the first week, commit to waiting 15 minutes before doing so. Increase the delay to 30 minutes during the following week. Then, for the week following that one, increase the delay to 60 minutes. This exercise will build your self-control. It'll also tell your brain that you're not at the mercy of your urges. You can exercise self-restraint.

4. Enjoy the feeling of being able to resist your urges. Knowing that you possess the self-discipline you need to control your responses to tempting stimuli is an empowering feeling. Appreciate it. Relish it. This self-discipline will

play a crucial role in helping you to achieve your goals, whether that entails being more productive, saving more money, or getting into shape.

5. Identify factors that make you more likely to seek instant gratification. These can be cognitive or environmental factors. For example, are you more inclined to watch television rather than work when you're feeling stressed? Are you more likely to overindulge in alcohol when you're around certain friends or in certain venues? Once you've identified the factors that influence your behavior, you can avoid them - at least until you're able to control your urges.

6. Forgive yourself when you stumble. You'll occasionally give in to your impulses despite every intention to refuse them. That's okay. Don't scold yourself. Recognize that occasional stumbles are inevitable. When they occur, simply acknowledge them, brush yourself off, and move forward. Everyone makes mistakes. Dwelling on them is unproductive.

Day 22

Stop Constantly Switching Between Tasks

We've become so accustomed to task switching that we hardly notice doing it. In fact, task switching seems necessary as our lives become ever busier. At the office, we're bombarded by text, emails, and phone calls, even as we try to handle the myriad responsibilities of our jobs. At home, our attention is split between our spouses, children, pets, and household chores, as well as our computers, televisions, phones, and other gadgets.

Many of us manage competing demands for our time and attention by performing multiple activities at once. We write emails while attending conference calls. We cook dinner while talking on the phone. We respond to texts while playing with our kids. In the process, we trick ourselves into thinking that we're master multitaskers. What's actually taking place is called *task switching*. It's a cognitive process during which our attentional resources shift between activities.

In some cases, this process is highly streamlined. An example is driving a vehicle. We look in our mirrors, monitor the road in front of us, check our speed, look for traffic lights, and watch our blind spots, all while steering and applying the gas or brakes. We *think* we're multitasking. But we're actually task switching. In this example, the adverse effects of task switching are unnoticeable because the process is so fluid due to repetition. (Most of us have been driving for years.)

Other times, task switching is highly inefficient. An example is cooking an unfamiliar meal while talking to our banks regarding a problem with our checking accounts. Here, the process is far less streamlined because the inputs we're required to give are more variable. The meal prep is unfamiliar to us and therefore demands more attention. The conversation with the bank representative is dynamic and likewise demands more attention. Trying to do both at once can quickly become problematic, producing disappointing results (e.g. a ruined meal, unasked questions, etc.).

Task switching is only highly streamlined in rare cases, namely those where the inputs are static and can be applied from muscle memory (e.g. driving a vehicle). Most of the time, it's highly inefficient and will severely limit your productivity.

How This Bad Habit Hurts Your Productivity

TASK SWITCHING PREVENTS you from achieving a flow state. Every switch is an interruption that inhibits your ability to "get in the zone," the mental state where you enjoy hyper focus and engagement. This is the state in which you produce your best work. It's also when you're most productive.

Task switching also slows you down. Recall the last time you were interrupted while working on something important. It probably took you significant time to get back on track. Research suggests it can take up to 25 minutes.[1] Because it takes so long to regain our momentum following interruptions, we end up taking longer than necessary to complete tasks.

Because task switching slows us down, we get less done. Have you ever looked at your to-do list at the end of the day and wondered why you accomplished so little? The problem may lie in the fact that you were repeatedly interrupted by phone calls, texts, and other distractions. If you were interrupted once every half hour, and it takes 25 minutes to get back on track, you can imagine the impact on your productivity.

Another problem with task switching is that it hampers our creativity. Creative thinking requires focus. If you're constantly switching from one task to another, you won't be able to fully concentrate on any one activity. Your attentional resources will shift too rapidly to achieve the single-minded focus needed to venture beyond conventional thinking. This will affect your ability to devise creative solutions to problems.

If you've ever monitored the way you work, you may have noticed that you switch tasks every few minutes.

Doing so may seem harmless, but in reality it's disastrous to your productivity. Here's how to break the cycle.

Action Steps

1. Start each day with a to-do list limited to seven items. This list will remind you of the day's top priorities. It alone won't discourage task switching. But it'll focus your attention on what you need to accomplish by the end of the day. This awareness is a crucial first step.

2. Close unnecessary browser tabs. A lot of task switching occurs because we see something online that catches our eye. We see articles that look interesting to us. We notice our friends have posted on Facebook. We spot news items that grab our attention. Before long, we have dozens of browser tabs open, each one a constant distraction. Close all of them except the ones you need to address the task at hand.

3. Turn off your phone. Notifications alerting you of incoming emails, texts, and phone calls can make it impossible to focus. Whenever you hear that you've received a message it's tempting to check it and fire off a quick response. While doing so may only require a few seconds, it's still an interruption. Your brain must shift your attentional resources from whatever you're

working on to address the new task. Instead, turn off your phone so you can avoid the distraction and temptation altogether.

4. Divide your day into time chunks. The duration of your time chunks should reflect your ability to focus. Keep in mind, this ability is like a muscle that becomes stronger with each use. If you're a habitual task switcher (i.e. multitasker), start with 10-minute time chunks. Commit to devoting yourself solely to the task at hand for these short periods. Once you're able to do so without difficulty, start scheduling 15-minute time chunks. After awhile, you'll be able to extend the time to 20 minutes, and then 30 minutes, and so on. Be sure to take short breaks between each time chunk.

5. Mind your health. Get sufficient sleep each night. For most people, that means eight hours. Some people function perfectly well with six hours. The important thing to keep in mind is that fatigue will make you more prone to distractions. Consequently, you'll be more susceptible to task switching. Also modify your diet to avoid hunger and cognitive slumps during the day. Sugary snacks may give you a quick boost of energy, but can lead to a crash later as your blood sugar levels plummet. And because the sugar enters your bloodstream so quickly, you may also experience hunger shortly

after eating. It's difficult to focus when you're hungry. High-protein foods, such as eggs, chicken breast, lentils, and Greek yogurt, will sustain you longer than sugary junk food.

[1] https://www.ics.uci.edu/~gmark/chi08-mark.pdf

Day 23

~

Stop Drowning Yourself In Information

WE NEED information to make good decisions. We also need it to take purposeful action with a reasonable expectation of success. Without good intel, we're forced to fly in the dark, guessing when we should be acting with confidence.

Here's the problem: it's easy to get into the habit of gathering *too much* information before moving forward. We immerse ourselves in it to gain confidence in our decisions. But this ultimately becomes a stalling tactic. We convince ourselves that gathering additional intel is beneficial, even when doing so yields little benefit. It becomes a way to rationalize procrastination.

I speak from experience. Years ago, when faced with a decision, I'd research every option, regardless of its feasibility. And I'd spend an inordinate amount of time doing so. Eventually, I realized this habit stemmed from fear. I was afraid to make a *wrong* decision or take a *wrong* action, so I buried myself in research to delay taking the risk.

I'll explain how I overcame this habit in a few

moments. But first, let's take a look at how drowning your-self in information hurts your productivity.

How This Bad Habit Hurts Your Productivity

THIS HABIT CRIPPLES your ability to get things done in three distinct ways. First, it hamstrings decision making. When you're presented with multiple options, it's easy to get bogged down investigating the potential repercussions of each of them. Such investigation may at first seem prudent. After all, the more intel you possess, the better your decision. But information gathering follows the law of diminishing returns. There comes a point at which the value of additional intel is outweighed by the cost of its collection. In such cases, this cost is measured in terms of wasted time and lost opportunities.

Second, information overload leads to analysis paraly-sis. We gather a mountain of intel to make better decisions and take better-informed action, but the opposite happens. We become paralyzed with indecision because the intel implies too many options. Rarely does all the information point to a single course of action as the perfect choice. Instead, we're presented with alternatives, each of which carries an opportunity cost. We fear making a poor choice, and this fear causes us to freeze and do nothing.

Third, information overload wastes time. It forces us to take more time than necessary to complete tasks because we're hampered by doubts. We want to make *perfect* decisions and take *perfect* actions given our options. We loathe moving forward with even a modicum of uncertainty. So we stall, hoping to avoid facing this predicament. But stalling only results in time slipping through our fingers, time that could have been put to more productive use.

It's easier than ever to fall into this trap these days because of the internet. Information is literally at our fingertips. Moreover, it's limitless, which aggravates the problem. You can spend all of your time researching options and never exhaust the supply of intel.

If you struggle with this tendency, I have good news. You *can* overcome it. Following is a quick and simple action plan for doing so.

Action Steps

1. Recognize that *more* information isn't always better. This is a pivotal first step. The tendency to overload ourselves with information stems from our mindset. We convince ourselves, usually due to our fear of the unknown, that more intel is better. This belief becomes deeply rooted in our minds to the point that we never question its veracity. So, acknowledge that *more* intel doesn't guarantee you'll make perfect decisions.

2. Get comfortable with the fact that every decision and every action imposes an opportunity cost. Choosing one option requires sacrificing benefits associated with other options. For example, suppose you intend to buy a new vehicle and need to choose between a sedan and SUV. You'll get better mileage with a sedan, but you'll sacrifice interior space, seating position and visibility, and crash safety (due to size). Once you accept that moving forward requires making sacrifices, you'll find it easier to do so with confidence.

3. Identify your main sources of information. Do you typically peruse certain websites to obtain the intel you deem valuable? Do you rely on direction from social media? Or do you reach out to people you know to be more knowledgeable than you regarding the decision at hand? None of these practices are imprudent in and of themselves. But they can become so if you're using them to stall for time. It's important to identify them so you can resist grasping for them when the time comes to act.

4. Set deadlines. Commit to making your decision or taking action by a certain time or date. Treat this deadline as sacrosanct. When it arrives, cut off your information sources and move forward with the intel you possess.

5. Train yourself to move forward with uncertainty. As is always the case in habit development, the key is to start small and build up gradually. Start by making inconsequential decisions without research. For example, visit restaurants for dinner without first checking their reviews on Yelp. Watch films without first checking their ratings on RottenTomatoes and MetaCritic. Over time, begin making more consequential decisions without doing an inordinate amount of research beforehand. For example, plan a weekend getaway with your spouse without choosing the "perfect" hotel. Join a local charity without investigating whether it aligns *perfectly* with your values. The purpose of this exercise is to desensitize yourself to taking decisive action when faced with doubts and uncertain outcomes.

6. Avoid informational crutches. These are information bytes that confirm what we already know. They're a form of validation. But because the validation is redundant, it offers negligible value. For example, suppose you need to choose a web hosting service for your website, and have narrowed your choices down to a single company. You're convinced this company is the right choice. But you may still be tempted to search online for reviews that

support this belief. At this point in the decision-making process, these reviews constitute informational crutches. They offer little value because they merely confirm what you already know.

≈

Stop Working Without Clearly-Defined Goals

I'M a strong advocate of setting personal and professional goals. In my opinion, doing so is what separates achievers from dreamers. While it's possible to accomplish big things and experience success *without* goals, both circumstances are more likely when clear, reasonable goals have been set.

Proper goal-setting involves creating action plans. That is, once we identify our desired outcome (e.g. lose 30 pounds, save $50,000, etc.), we formulate a plan, complete with benchmarks, to make it happen. For example, we might plan to lose two pounds a week or save $500 a month. As long as we're meeting our benchmarks, we can have confidence that we'll succeed in achieving our desired outcome.

When we work *without* goals, it's difficult to know whether we're on the right track. For example, suppose you manage employees who produce widgets. Let's say you'd like to improve your employees' productivity by 15%, either in terms of higher production or fewer errors. Unless you create goals and benchmarks by which to measure these things, you'll lack a way to gauge success.

Many people believe they've set personal and professional goals, but in fact they've only identified their aspirations. For example, they aspire to learn a new language, type faster, or read more non-fiction. But they neglect to clearly define their desired outcomes (e.g. watch French films without needing subtitles, type 100 words per minute, or read three non-fiction books each month). Without defining such outcomes, it's impossible to create plans to bring them to pass.

If you're guilty of this type of neglect, you're almost certainly limiting your productivity.

How This Bad Habit Hurts Your Productivity

When we work without goals, we do so without clarity regarding what we hope to achieve. For example, we save money, but are unsure how much money we should save. We practice typing, but are unable to tell when we've achieved proficiency. We exercise, but because we're uncertain whether to focus on losing weight, building stamina, or increasing muscle mass, we're uncertain regarding which routines to perform. Without knowing what we'd like to achieve, we waste time and energy.

This habit also removes the impetus to take action. If we neglect to identify our desired outcome, and further neglect to create an action plan with benchmarks and deadlines, there's no urgency to act. Without this urgency, it's easy to become lethargic. We end up procrastinating instead of taking action.

Goals gives us purpose and a sense of control over our lives. When we take purposeful action, we enjoy a feeling of empowerment. When this action results in meeting benchmarks, we enjoy a sense of achievement. These feelings do more than improve our general outlook. They motivate us to continue striving for positive results. Our goals and benchmarks serve as evidence of our self-efficacy.

Working without clearly-defined goals also obstructs our ability to make good decisions. Our options and their respective opportunity costs become vague, making it more difficult for us to choose from among them. For example, suppose you're saving money, but neglect to set a savings goal (e.g. $10,000). Without this goal in place, decisions regarding how to spend your discretionary income become unnecessarily complicated. You can't ask yourself, *"Which choice gets me closer to my goal?"* because no clearly-defined goal exists.

Lastly, the absence of goals eliminates accountability. If we're not following an action plan nor striving to meet predetermined benchmarks, there's no evidence of failure. Thus, we cannot hold ourselves responsible for lack of achievement. This circumstance poses a drawback because accountability presents numerous benefits. It spurs us to take action, keeps us focused on our deadlines, and compels us to stick to our commitments. When we're not accountable, these motivations are too easily abandoned.

Setting goals may seem daunting if you've never done it. But it's simple if you follow the right strategy. Moreover, the more often you do it, the easier it becomes.

Action Steps

1. Start with small goals. The purpose is to train yourself to set goals without the pressure of achieving *big* goals. For example, rather than setting a goal to lose 50 pounds, set a goal to lose eight pounds. Then create an action plan with benchmarks - for example, "lose two pounds per week." Achieving goals, even small ones, causes the brain to release dopamine (a neurotransmitter). This feel-good hormone is associated with a sense of euphoria, which encourages us to continue doing that which resulted in its release.

2. Create S.M.A.R.T. goals. This acronym stands for **S**pecific, **M**easurable, **A**chievable, **R**elevant, and **T**ime-sensitive. Essentially, a goal should be clearly-defined, involve items that can be measured (e.g. volume, dates, etc.), reasonable, consistent with your aspirations, and accompanied by a deadline. The S.M.A.R.T. goal-setting method is imperfect. But it's a good place to start because it's straightforward.

3. Rank your goals according to their priority.

Some will be more important to you than others. Some will be more urgent than others, warranting your attention in the present. Ranking them by priority will reveal where you should allocate your resources.

4. Set daily goals. These can be as simple as "meditate for 10 minutes," "do 20 pushups," or "write in my journal." That is, these daily goals can be represented by simple to-do list items. The purpose of this exercise is not to get through your daily to-do list. Rather, it's to help you to develop the goal-setting *habit*. Doing so will gradually change your mindset. You'll eventually regard everything you want to achieve in the context of taking intentional action to meet predefined benchmarks. This is an incredibly-empowering attitude.

5. Review your progress once a week. Evaluate your performance. Did you satisfy your daily goals during the past week? Did you meet the benchmarks associated with your longer-term goals? Did you spend your time wisely in that regard? If you failed in any of these areas, try to determine the reasons (insufficient time, excessive workload, lack of support, etc.). This is also a good time to revisit whether your goals are still relevant. Some goals become irrelevant due to circumstances. For example, suppose you aspire to take your family on a long vacation

over the summer. But you receive a big promotion at your job that precludes your taking the time off. In this scenario, your new time constraint makes the goal impossible, and therefore irrelevant.

Day 25

~

Stop Waiting For The Perfect Time To Act

"*Now's not a good time.*"

You've probably said this in the past, either to yourself or someone else. Maybe you used it as an excuse to avoid committing to something you expected to be unpleasant. Perhaps you said it as a way to delay taking action. You hoped for circumstances to align in a way that would optimize your results.

For example, suppose you want to advance your career. Let's also suppose that doing so will require looking for a position with a different employer, a considerable challenge to the status quo. As a stalling tactic, you might be tempted to tell yourself, "*Now's not a good time.*" This gives you implicit permission to do nothing.

Or let's say you'd like to start a side business. You're motivated by the thought of earning extra income each month. And who knows? This new venture may grow large enough to support you and your family, allowing you to quit your job. But starting a business, even one that you run from the corner of your bedroom, involves a lot of moving parts. Daunted, you may be tempted to tell yourself, "*Now's not a good time.*"

Waiting for circumstances to align perfectly before you take action may seem sensible. But it's important to realize there will *never* be a perfect time to act. Challenges will always exist. This being the case, waiting for the perfect moment is, in reality, a form of procrastination.

How This Bad Habit Hurts Your Productivity

FIRST, waiting makes us complacent. It trains us be satisfied with the status quo. Rather than tackling new challenges, we become content to revel in our past accomplishments. For example, a salesperson might savor the recognition he received for meeting last month's sales goals, and put in less effort to meet *this* month's sales goals. A college student might be so pleased with her performance on a recent exam that she neglects to study sufficiently for an *upcoming* exam. Complacency not only hampers our personal and professional growth, but it also constrains our productivity.

Second, waiting for the perfect time to act results in missed opportunities. It trains us to think of opportunities as occasions where we stand to benefit without risk. We adopt the mindset that all we need to do to take advantage of the opportunities is to accept them. But that's rarely how life works. Opportunities are not lottery tickets. They're accompanied by risk (risk of failure, risk of time wasted, etc.). Refusing to accept such risk as a condition of pursuing opportunities is akin to refusing to pursue them altogether.

Third, waiting puts our goals on perpetual hold. Because circumstances never align perfectly, waiting for the perfect time to act essentially means we never take action. Consequently, we fail to realize our aspirations, all of which require us to take purposeful action.

If you've gotten into the habit of waiting for circumstances to align perfectly before acting, now's the time to make a change. The upside is, taking action without waiting for the perfect moment will boost your productivity and ultimately lead to a more rewarding life.

Action Steps

1. Recognize that there is never a perfect time to act. It's one thing to read the claim in a book about personal development. It's another thing entirely to accept it as truth. Acceptance is complicated by the fact that waiting for the perfect moment is, for many of us, a deeply-rooted habit. It's an entrenched behavioral pattern. Recognizing the fallacy that encourages it is critical to *breaking* the pattern.

2. Develop disdain for the status quo. There's nothing wrong with being comfortable and proud with your current state in life. Indeed, it's

important to reflect on our accomplishments because they're evidence that we control the trajectory of our lives. At the same time, it's equally important to continually improve ourselves. Doing so has a profound impact on our long-term happiness. The problem is, the pursuit of self-improvement challenges the status quo, the brain's preferred state. So expect to encounter internal resistance whenever you seek to change the latter. One way to adopt a growth-oriented mindset, one that disapproves of the status quo, is to take on new challenges whenever they present themselves.

3. Take small actions when circumstances are out of your favor. Doing so will gradually desensitize your brain to the risk of acting when circumstances are less than ideal. Small actions are associated with limited consequences. For example, suppose you're waiting for the "perfect" time to pitch a potential client. Stop waiting. Call the client and make your pitch. What's the worst that can happen? (The potential client will say no.) Or let's say you're waiting for the "perfect" time to take your spouse on a weekend getaway. Stop waiting. Plan it and enjoy it. Again, what's the worst that can happen? (You're bound to enjoy the getaway, even if the timing is less than perfect.) We're training the mind to recognize that

intentions are only valuable if we're willing to take action to fulfill them. And waiting for the perfect time to act is merely a form of procrastination.

4. Increase the stakes. Developing the habit of taking action despite imperfect circumstances is like building a muscle. Repetition and resistance are crucial. The more often you "exercise" the habit, and the more resistance you overcome in doing so, the stronger the habit becomes. In the previous step, we took small actions to desensitize ourselves to the risks inherent in acting without waiting. In this step, take progressively larger actions, ones that lead to bigger potential rewards, but also carry bigger risks. For example, start looking for the new position that'll catapult your career. Launch the side business you've been mulling over for the last several months. If you've been thinking about moving, call a real estate agent to list your home for sale. Bigger actions, bigger potential rewards, and bigger risks. This is a vital part of accepting that waiting for the perfect moment to act only prevents you from moving forward.

Stop Using Unnecessary Productivity Apps

NEW PRODUCTIVITY TOOLS are difficult to resist. They promise to make us more efficient and effective, helping us to get more stuff done in less time. And they all claim to offer the crucial piece of the puzzle that we've been missing. If you're like me, always looking for ways to be more productive, this is a heady pledge. It's easy to feel as if you're missing out if you neglect to at least *try* the new tool. The fact that you're already using an app that serves the same purpose is irrelevant.

For example, I've used Google Calendar for years. It's simple, intuitive, and free. But every time a new calendar app (e.g. Fantastical 2, Calendars 5, CloudCal, etc.) is released, I'm tempted to try it. And eventually, I end up maintaining multiple calendar apps, which is a complete waste of time (ironic). I'm the same way with note-taking apps. I've happily used Evernote for years. But other note-taking apps, such as OneNote, Notes, and Zoho Notebook, call to me. And new ones are especially tempting simply because they're new.

Here's the problem: the inclination to use new productivity apps inevitably leads to redundancy. We end up maintaining multiple calendars, to-do lists, note-taking apps, and address books, many of which share the features that are important to us. This hurts our productivity in numerous ways.

How This Bad Habit Hurts Your Productivity

First, using redundant apps results in confusion. For example, suppose you use Evernote to keep track of household projects, bills, car maintenance details, and various workflows. Suppose you decide to try OneNote. You begin adding notes to the app concerning household expenses, business ideas, and travel plans. And after hearing good things about MyScript Nebo, you start using *that* app, too. This continues until one day you need to review details about a particular client. Unfortunately, you're unable to remember which platform you used to store those notes. You're now forced to waste time searching for them in multiple apps.

Second, using unnecessary productivity tools makes us more vulnerable to distraction. We fiddle with the tools, testing their features, without actually completing to-do items and advancing projects. We rationalize that we're investigating apps that can make a measurable difference in our daily productivity. But in truth, we waste valuable time scrutinizing tools for which we have no need. We end up sacrificing our focus, which makes it more difficult for us to complete important work.

Third, jumping at every new productivity app trains us to think of such apps as the cornerstones of our productivity. We slowly convince ourselves that we'd languish without them - that we're incapable of getting things done without their aid. But in reality, that's nonsense. Productivity tools are merely *tools*. They help us to optimize our current processes. If these processes aren't already in place, the apps are useless to us.

For example, if I were not in the habit of using a calendar as a planning tool, it wouldn't matter whether I aspired to use Google Calendar, Fantastical 2, or Cloud-Cal. These apps would be ineffectual to me. From another perspective, because I *am* in the habit of using a calendar, it wouldn't matter if such apps were unavailable. I'd simply use a paper calendar to the same effect.

Productivity apps are not the reason we're productive. They merely help us leverage our productivity-related habits. With that in mind, if you constantly find yourself seduced by new productivity tools, here are several tips for resisting the temptation.

Action Steps

1. Commit to the "Law Of One" with respect to using productivity apps. Use one calendar app.

Use one note-taking app. Use one to-do list app. Use one time-tracking app.

2. Audit your current usage of productivity tools. Write down the apps you've installed on your phone and browser. If you're also using paper-based tools, such as a Moleskine or Franklin planner, make a note of them as well. Determine which ones you use most often. If you're using multiple apps per purpose (i.e. you're violating the "Law of One"), determine the reason. Does one of the apps offer a specific feature that's unavailable in the other app? Is one app more intuitive to use than the other app?

3. Consolidate your productivity tools. In cases where you're using multiple apps per purpose, note which features are most important to you and choose the one that offers them. If you're using features that are only independently available on the otherwise-redundant apps, ask yourself whether you truly need them. You'll likely find you can abandon them without consequence.

4. Ignore reviews of new productivity tools. Such reviews will only tempt you to try the tools. For our purposes, reading them is akin to being on a diet while carrying your favorite candy bar in your pocket. Avoid the temptation altogether.

5. Use apps that sync to each other. This will help

you to streamline your processes, bridge time-wasting gaps, and see a larger view of your day (or week, month, etc.). For example, I use Todoist to maintain my to-do lists. This tool syncs with Google Calendar. The integration of these two tools allows me to automatically add events on my calendar to my Todoist dashboard, and vice versa.

6. Purge the tools you no longer need. Identifying redundancies among your productivity apps is important. It's equally important to take the next logical step: getting rid of them. Uninstall them from your phone and browser. That way, you won't be tempted to fiddle with them nor reintegrate them into your bare-boned "Law of One" suite of productivity apps.

～

Stop Trying To Keep Everything In Your Head

IF YOU'RE KEEPING all of your to-do items in your head, things are almost certainly falling through the cracks. Perhaps you're missing appointments. Maybe you're forgetting to pick up certain grocery items. Or perhaps you're overlooking important tasks at your job.

The brain possesses working memory to store information for short-term processing. But this resource is limited. Information can be easily lost unless it's recorded.

That's the purpose of to-do lists. They allow you to dump all of the information swimming around in your brain onto a medium that precludes your having to remember it all. Doing so not only frees up your working memory, but it helps to ensure that items won't fall through the cracks. With a proper task management system in place, you can have confidence that your time and attention are spent where they'll have the greatest impact.

Having said that, you may still be tempted to rely on your memory, if only on occasion. Committing miscellaneous items (e.g. phone numbers, dates, etc.) to memory might seem more expedient since you'll avoid "wasting" time writing them down. But you'll find that doing so can ruin your productivity in the long run.

How This Bad Habit Hurts Your Productivity

I MENTIONED above that to-do items invariably fall through the cracks when we try to keep them in our heads. The brain's working memory is insufficient for remembering all of the details we need to track. Before long, we start to forget things. This can affect every area of our lives, from our jobs and relationships to our health and households.

Keeping everything in your head can also make you feel overwhelmed. You're probably juggling a large number of tasks, projects, and other responsibilities. Some are accompanied by deadlines. Some carry a risk of terrible consequences if you forget to address them (e.g. neglecting to pick up your child from school). It's easy to feel overwhelmed, buried under everything you need to do during the course of your day.

Relying on your memory also makes it difficult to prioritize to-do items. It's hard enough to remember every task, project, and responsibility. Committing their respective priorities to memory is infeasible. Without prioritization, it's difficult to know how and where to spend your limited time and attention.

When you neglect to write things down, you also become more prone to distraction. All of the information in your head eats away at your focus as trivial items compete with important items for your attention. This problem, which stems from a lack of prioritization, makes concentration difficult. It prevents you from entering a flow state, where you'd otherwise experience a high level of performance and productivity.

If you're unaccustomed to maintaining to-do lists, doing so may seem like a formidable task. It's easier than you might imagine. It's just a matter of developing a few small habits. Following is a quick-and-dirty action plan for making the change and becoming more organized and productive in the process.

Action Steps

1. Choose a medium that aligns with your preferences. I use Todoist. OneNote or Evernote may be more to your liking based on their respective features and layouts. Or you might decide to stick to paper. It's entirely up to you. Moreover, you can always switch to a different medium down the road.

2. Spend 10 minutes each day getting information out of your head. Think of this exercise as a daily brain dump. Write down everything onto a single list. Don't worry about organization. You'll address that task in the following Action Step. Pick a time of day that works well for you and stick to it. I conduct my daily brain dumps

at 9:00 p.m. You may prefer doing them while having breakfast.

3. Once you have every item on a single list, highlight those that need attention today (or tomorrow if you're doing this exercise in the evening). Assign them to your daily to-do list. I'll show you what to do with the others in Action Step #5.

4. Limit your daily to-do list to 10 items. Ideally, your list would have only seven items (or even fewer) as shorter lists improve your focus and motivation. But this may be impractical if your day is busy. In that case, consider 10 to be the maximum.

5. Maintain multiple lists. In addition to your daily to-do list, keep a "tiny task" list, a "recurring task" list, and as many project lists as necessary. A "tiny task" list should include small tasks that need your attention, but can be addressed in the future (i.e. not today). Examples include buying a birthday present for a friend, calling your parents, and taking your vehicle into the shop for an oil change. A "recurring task" list might include items such as mowing the lawn, paying bills, and creating a weekly sales report for your boss. Project lists should include action items associated with specific projects. For example, suppose you're writing a novel. A project list for this endeavor might include tasks such as "hire

an editor," "hire a cover designer," and "contact my agent to seek a publishing deal." There are other types of lists you can maintain, but these four are enough to get you started.

6. Assign priorities to every item on your daily to-do list, "tiny task" list, and project lists. Consider both urgency and importance (some tasks are urgent, but unimportant, and vice versa). I recommend you use a 1-2-3 or A-B-C protocol. It simplifies prioritization and produces the same advantages as more complicated protocols.

Day 28

～

Stop Letting Non-Essential Tasks Creep Onto Your Daily To-Do List

IMAGINE THIS SCENARIO: you start the day with a reasonably small to-do list. You're motivated to get through it and cross off every item. You're inspired to make the best use of your time, completing important tasks and advancing important projects.

But then something strange happens. As your day progresses, new tasks appear on your to-do list. You started the day with fewer than ten tasks, but are now facing dozens. Worse, most of the new items are unimportant to you. They're distractions more than anything else. And worst of all, whereas you started the day feeling motivated and inspired, you now feel discouraged and apathetic.

How did this happen?

The busyness of our live is constant. During every waking hour, we're confronted by a stream of new demands for our attentional resources. Some of these demands stem from our responsibilities. Others are borne of other people's needs and wants. Whatever their origin, it's tempting to add these demands, in the form of new to-do items, to our lists. The smaller the demands, the greater the temptation because we infer that addressing them will require minimal time and effort.

The reality is, this habit of adding non-essential tasks to our daily to-do lists cripples our productivity and effectiveness.

How This Bad Habit Hurts Your Productivity

WHEN WE ALLOW inconsequential to-do items to creep onto our daily to-do lists, we end up spending time on low-value work. These items may seem harmless, especially if they require little time. But given that our time is limited, they redirect crucial resources away from high-value work, the type that's more likely to advance our goals.

For example, suppose you're working on an important presentation for your boss. This is a high-priority project that's accompanied by an aggressive deadline. While you're working, a coworker asks that you help her later in the day with a report. It's tempting to agree to help, adding the item to your to-do list. The problem is, doing so may impact you later if preparing your presentation takes more time than you anticipated. Worse, if that's the case, you'll be abandoning high-value work to attend to low-value work (low-value to you, at least).

Allowing extraneous items onto your daily to-do lists

also depletes your focus. When your lists contain fewer than 10 tasks, you can devote your attentional resources to them without significant distraction. But this changes when your lists grow to include dozens of low-value tasks. You become pulled in too many directions, many of which have conflicting priorities and objectives. This shatters your focus.

This bad habit is inconspicuous, and thus develops without our realization. We allow our daily to-do lists to grow without full awareness that it's happening. And unless we scrutinize its effect, we're certain to overlook how it negatively impacts our productivity. Let's put a stop to it, and in doing so reclaim our valuable and limited attentional resources.

Action Steps

1. Associate every to-do list item with a personal or professional goal. This exercise will help you to distinguish high-value work from low-value work. Tasks that are associated with your desired outcomes should be considered important. Tasks that are *unassociated* with your desired outcomes should be considered *unimportant.*

2. Avoid unimportant work. Important work moves you towards your goals. Because your attentional resources are limited, you must

carefully guard them. Maximizing your productivity requires that you spend these resources where they'll have the greatest impact. And *that* means dropping non-essential items from your to-do list.

3. Start saying no. There will never be a shortage of people who want you to help them. Meanwhile, your time and attention are constantly in short supply. Your job is to allocate these resources judiciously. Doing so requires that you set boundaries, and that means growing accustomed to saying no to people. The alternative (saying yes) ultimately leads to being burdened with others' demands, and allowing those demands to clutter and lengthen your to-do list.

4. Maintain a "do not do" list. This is a list of tasks and activities you've identified as not worth your time, and therefore important to avoid. Examples include constantly checking email, answering phone calls without recognizing the callers, and automatically saying yes to people. Avoiding these activities will allow you to better focus on what truly matters to you. It'll prevent you from wasting your time, increasing your productivity in the process.

5. Distinguish between urgent and important tasks. We discussed the difference in *Day 15*, so

we won't rehash the details here. Suffice to repeat that urgent tasks may be irrelevant to your goals, and thus unimportant. That being the case, you can confidently ignore or delegate without consequence.

~

Stop Assigning Too Much Gravity To Email

EMAIL DOESN'T DEGRADE our productivity. On the contrary, email can *boost* our productivity. The problem is, many of us have developed bad habits when it comes to reading and responding to emails.

For example, we try to be hyper-responsive. We check for new messages every few minutes and rush to reply shortly after new ones arrive. Or worse, we set up a notification that alerts us to new emails. This alleviates the need to check every few minutes, but the constant chirps and beeps of the alerts destroy our focus.

Another bad habit is checking email in the morning. This can result in a time suck, consuming precious time when our energy levels are high and we're able to have the greatest impact on high-value work. To be sure, some folks must check email in the morning due to their jobs and other obligations. But most of us can postpone doing so until the afternoon or evening.

Another email practice that wastes time is writing responses that are too lengthy. I'm guilty of this myself. Few emails we receive warrant more than a few sentences in response. Jeff Bezos, founder of Amazon, famously writes ultra-short emails to those who report to him. Some are as short as "?," sent by Bezos to executives when he learns of customer-related issues.

These habits are borne of our tendency to give email too much weight. We consider every message we receive to be important and urgent when, in truth, the majority are neither.

How This Bad Habit Hurts Your Productivity

TREATING email with such great consequence affects your productivity in four ways. First, it wastes time. Checking repeatedly for new emails, and replying immediately to them, pulls you away from other tasks and projects.

Second, it ruins your focus. If you're constantly checking for - and replying to - new emails, you'll never enjoy the momentum that allows you to reach a flow state. I mentioned in *Day 7* that it takes the brain more than 20 minutes to get back on track following a single interruption. Consider that in the context of checking and replying to email every few minutes.

Third, it becomes a source of anxiety. We start to fret about messages that are waiting for our attention in our inboxes. This concern siphons our attentional resources from more productive pursuits.

Fourth, email begins to consume our time outside "normal" email hours. For example, we lay in bed at night responding to emails when we should be winding down and getting ready to sleep. We spend time replying to emails on the weekends, preventing us from being present with our families and friends.

Treating email with too much gravity has another adverse effect: it influences others' expectations regarding our responsiveness. If we reply immediately to new messages, recipients learn to expect us to continue doing so. This becomes a stress-inducing trap of our own making.

Following is a game plan for turning email from a time-wasting effort into a tool that increases your productivity. Some of the steps may seem counterintuitive. They may also challenge your impulses. But if you incorporate them into your day, I guarantee you'll get more important work done.

Action Steps

1. Turn off email notifications. If you've set up an alert that interrupts you whenever new messages arrive, shut it off.

2. Choose two times of the day to check email (I recommended this practice in *Day 7*). For example, check for new messages at 11:00 a.m. and 5:00 p.m. These check-in times should dovetail with your circumstances. If possible, try to keep your mornings email-free

as they're likely to comprise your most productive hours.

3. Assign time chunks for checking and responding to email. For example, you might allocate 20 minutes for each session. The duration will depend on your circumstances. The idea is to limit the time you spend by recognizing Parkinson's law ("work expands so as to fill the time available for its completion").

4. Check and respond to email when your energy levels are low. An example might be right after you eat lunch. By doing so, you'll find it easier to resist the temptation to become overly invested in each email and response. You'll also be less tempted to reply to emails that don't require your doing so.

5. Commit to avoiding email during the late evenings and weekends. While emergencies are possible, they're rare. Moreover, if someone truly needs your immediate attention, they're likely to text and/or call you.

6. Delete or archive with abandon. I learned years ago, while working in Corporate America, that only a minority percentage of emails require responses. To be sure, everyone *wants* a response. But responses are often unnecessary. You can delete or archive the emails without consequence. This may be difficult to do in the beginning. After all, you're denying your own

tendencies while simultaneously challenging others' expectations. The more you do it, however, the easier it gets. And if you approach this new practice with grace, explaining to coworkers and friends that you're trying to be more productive, you'll find most will be receptive and understanding. Some, struggling with their own email loads, may even express empathy.

7. Ask others to call you if their needs are urgent. Doing so will adjust their expectations with regard to your responsiveness to their emails. It'll let them know that you're available (even if you decide to say no to their requests later) while conveying your desire to control your time.

8. Limit emails to five sentences. Doing so will help you to reply to emails more quickly. And you'll find that few recipients will take issue with your brevity. Many will even be thankful for it. Keep in mind, brevity isn't an excuse for vagueness. To make this work, your responses should contain necessary details. Just be concise. It may help to remember that many people scan the emails they receive rather than reading them. Conciseness helps all parties.

∽

Stop Allowing Yourself To Get Derailed From Your Goals

OUR GOALS SHOULD COMPEL us to act. They should encourage us to commit to pursuits we might otherwise abandon. They meld our long-term aspirations with our present practices, motivating us to replace our bad habits with better ones.

For example, suppose you want to learn to speak a new language. Speaking a new language fluently can take years, making this a long-term goal. The only way to bring it to pass is to devote attention to it in the present. This means setting aside time each day to practice new words and phrases and overcome the idiosyncratic challenges presented by the language to non-native speakers.

Or suppose you'd like to launch a side business that generates extra income each month. Building the business to the point that it generates regular income may take several months. Along the way, you'll need to create a product or service, design a marketing strategy, build a website, and incorporate a payment solution (and that's just the beginning). There are a lot of moving parts, and daily action is necessary to keep on top of them.

Unfortunately, it's easy to get distracted from our goals. We're bombarded with stimuli each day, from the moment we get out of bed in the morning until the moment we climb back into bed in the evening. It's tempting to set aside the habits that lead to goal achievement to cater to our immediate, and presumably more gratifying, impulses.

But if we do so, we risk wrecking our productivity and sabotaging our forward progress.

How This Bad Habit Hurts Your Productivity

CONSIDER the attributes that make it possible for us to achieve our goals. Whether we're learning a new language, launching a side business, or pursuing a promotion at work, they're homogeneous. They include diligence, grit, and focus. They include attention to detail, the ability to say no to others, and an interest in continual personal growth.

Notice that these attributes are highly consistent among folks who are regularly able to complete large volumes of important work. Think of ultra-productive people you know. There's a good chance they exhibit the above traits.

When we create goals, we implicitly commit to developing and maintaining these traits. They're inherent in the habits and routines we adopt. The only way we can get *derailed* from our goals is if we abandon them. For example, we stop being diligent, choosing to play rather than work. We allow Facebook, Netflix, and Youtube to ruin our focus.

We relax our custom of saying no to others, allowing their needs and wants to supersede our own.

These choices - and it's important to recognize them as such - hobble our productivity. They whittle away our attentional resources, leaving us with little with which to attend to important, high-value work.

Perhaps you set goals long ago that you abandoned at some point in your life. Maybe you still intend to pursue them, but are finding it difficult to get back on track. Or perhaps you're in the early stages of goal achievement, and fear losing your way due to the myriad of distractions that surround you. Following is a quick action plan that'll help you to avoid goal derailment, or get back on track if you've already strayed off course.

Action Steps

1. Consider the reasons you want to achieve the goal in question. You didn't set the goal in a vacuum. Something motivated you to do so. What was that motivation? For example, do you aspire to speak fluent Mandarin because you plan to live in Hong Kong, where Mandarin is the official language? Do you want to launch a side business to generate income you can use for family vacations? Reminding ourselves of our motivations keeps us focused.

2. Break down your goals. Set milestones and deadlines. Then, identify daily actions that'll help you to achieve them. For example, you may decide to master a vocabulary list composed of 250 phrases by the end of the month. You might estimate that doing so will require you to practice for 30 minutes per day. Think of every goal as an amalgamation of milestones, deadlines, and daily actions. Doing so will transform your goals from mere dreams to achievable ambitions.

3. Add the daily actions to your to-do list and calendar. Schedule time chunks to address them during your day so you won't forget them. For example, you might schedule your 30-minute Mandarin sessions for 6:30 p.m. to 7:00 p.m. Put that time chunk on your calendar to prevent other activities from encroaching upon that time slot.

4. Develop hyperfocus. Commit to ignoring *everything* except your identified daily actions during the assigned time chunk. For example, between 6:30 p.m. and 7:00 p.m., occupy an isolated room in your home, close the door, and turn off your phone. The sharper your focus, the greater your effectiveness.

5. Pare down unnecessary activities and unjustified obligations. As we've noted

repeatedly, your time and energy are limited resources. It's important to conserve them for high-value work and the ongoing pursuit of your goals. If you typically watch eight hours of Netflix per day, trim down this time investment. If you normally drive your friend to work each morning, reconsider whether you want to continue shouldering that obligation. If you're uncertain where your time is being spent, track it for two weeks using Toggl, Clockify, or TimeCamp.

6. Wake up an hour earlier. Admittedly, this isn't for everyone. Some people do their most productive work while burning the midnight oil. For most of us, however, getting up earlier increases our productivity (assuming we enjoy quality sleep). I recommend waking up earlier in small increments. For example, suppose you normally wake up at 6:00 a.m. Spend a few days getting up 5:50 a.m. Spend the next few days getting up at 5:40 a.m. Then 5:30 a.m., 5:20 a.m., and so on, until you reach your desired waking time.

7. Prioritize daily actions and their accompanying milestones over the goals with which they're associated. Using our earlier example, let's say you want to learn to speak fluent Mandarin. It's important to keep that goal in mind as well as your motivations for achieving it. But it's *more*

important to focus on your 30-minute Mandarin practice sessions (daily action) and mastery of the aforementioned 250-phrase vocabulary list (milestone). These items are in your direct control.

FINAL THOUGHTS ON THE 30-DAY
PRODUCTIVITY PLAN - VOLUME II

∼

T hroughout this book, I've prioritized actionable tips over theory. In my opinion, too much time spent on theory makes it easier to get lost in the weeds. Taking *purposeful* action is the crucial ingredient in achieving personal growth, and theory isn't necessary to that end.

It's also my opinion that cheerleading is next to useless. To be sure, encouragement and inspiration are important, and I've tried to provide both in this book at appropriate times. But at some point - and it's usually earlier than later - cheerleading start to take away from the actionable material that can transform your life.

With these two things in mind, I hope you'll put to use

the 30 miniature action plans found throughout this book. If you do so, I'm confident you'll see remarkable, inspiring changes in your habits and routines that'll set the stage for immense gratification in the long run.

MAY I ASK YOU A SMALL FAVOR?

∼

First and foremost, thank you for taking the time to read *The 30-Day Productivity Plan - Volume II*. I realize your time is limited and consider it an honor that you've spent it with me in these pages. I hope the experience was a rewarding one.

If anything in this book resonated with you, I'd love it if you would leave a review for the book on Amazon. Reviews may not matter to big-name authors like David Allen, Timothy Ferriss, and Ray Dalio, but they're a *tremendous* help for little guys like myself. They help me to grow my readership by encouraging folks to take a chance on my books.

Second, if you'd like to be notified when I release new

books (typically at a steep discount), please sign up for my mailing list at:

http://artofproductivity.com/free-gift/

You'll receive immediate access to my 40-page PDF guide *Catapult Your Productivity: The Top 10 Habits You Must Develop To Get More Things Done.* You'll also receive actionable advice on beating procrastination, creating morning routines, avoiding burnout, developing razor-sharp focus, and more!

If you have questions or would like to share a productivity tip that has made a measurable difference in your life, please feel free to reach out to me at damon@artofproductivity.com. I'd love to hear from you!

Until next time,

Damon Zahariades
http://artofproductivity.com

OTHER BOOKS BY DAMON ZAHARIADES

∽

The P.R.I.M.E.R. Goal Setting Method: The Only Goal Achievement Guide You'll Ever Need!

An elegant 6-step system for achieving extraordinary results in every area of your life!

∽

80/20 Your Life! How To Get More Done With Less Effort And Change Your Life In The Process!

Achieve more, create more, and enjoy more success - while taking less action! It's time to 80/20 your life!

∽

The Joy Of Imperfection: A Stress-Free Guide To Silencing Your Inner Critic, Conquering Perfectionism, and Becoming The Best Version Of Yourself!

Is perfectionism causing you to feel stressed, irritated, and chronically unhappy? Here's how to silence your inner critic, embrace imperfection, and live without fear!

~

The Art Of Saying NO: How To Stand Your Ground, Reclaim Your Time And Energy, And Refuse To Be Taken For Granted (Without Feeling Guilty!)

Are you fed up with people taking you for granted? Learn how to set boundaries, stand your ground, and inspire others' respect in the process!

~

The Procrastination Cure: 21 Proven Tactics For Conquering Your Inner Procrastinator, Mastering Your Time, And Boosting Your Productivity!

Do you struggle with procrastination? Discover how to take quick action, make fast decisions, and finally overcome your inner procrastinator!

~

Morning Makeover: How To Boost Your Productivity, Explode Your Energy, and Create An Extraordinary Life - One Morning At A Time!

Would you like to start each day on the right foot? Here's how to create quality morning routines that set you up for more daily success!

~

Fast Focus: A Quick-Start Guide To Mastering Your Attention, Ignoring Distractions, And Getting More Done In Less Time!

Are you constantly distracted? Does your mind wander after just a few minutes? Learn how to develop laser-sharp focus!

~

Small Habits Revolution: 10 Steps To Transforming Your Life Through The Power Of Mini Habits!

Got 5 minutes a day? Use this simple, effective plan for creating any new habit you desire!

~

The 30-Day Productivity Plan: Break The 30 Bad Habits That Are Sabotaging Your Time Management - One Day At A Time!

Need a daily action plan to boost your productivity? This 30-day guide is the solution to your time management woes!

~

The Time Chunking Method: A 10-Step Action Plan For Increasing Your Productivity

It's one of the most popular time management strategies used today. Double your productivity with this easy 10-step system.

Digital Detox: The Ultimate Guide To Beating Technology Addiction, Cultivating Mindfulness, and Enjoying More Creativity, Inspiration, And Balance In Your Life!

Are you addicted to Facebook and Instagram? Are you obsessed with your phone? Use this simple, step-by-step plan to take a technology vacation!

For a complete list, please visit

http://artofproductivity.com/my-books/

ABOUT THE AUTHOR

Damon Zahariades is a corporate refugee who endured years of unnecessary meetings, drive-by chats with coworkers, and a distraction-laden work environment before striking out on his own. Today, in addition to being the author of a growing catalog of time management and productivity books, he's the showrunner for the productivity blog ArtofProductivity.com.

In his spare time, he shows off his copywriting chops by powering the content marketing campaigns used by today's growing businesses to attract customers.

Damon lives in Southern California with his beautiful, supportive wife and their frisky dog. He's currently staring down the barrel of his 50th birthday.

www.artofproductivity.com

Printed in Great Britain
by Amazon